BUILDER OF ALL THINGS

Copyright © 2025 by Richie Breaux

Published by AVAIL

All rights reserved. No portion of this book may be reproduced, stored in a retrieval system, or transmitted in any form or by any means—electronic, mechanical, photocopy, recording, scanning, or other—except for brief quotations in critical reviews or articles, without prior written permission of the author.

Unless otherwise noted, all Scripture quotations are taken from the Holy Bible, New International Version®, NIV®. Copyright © 1973, 1978, 1984, 2011 by Biblica, Inc.™ Used by permission of Zondervan. All rights reserved worldwide. www.zondervan.com. The "NIV" and "New International Version" are trademarks registered in the United States Patent and Trademark Office by Biblica, Inc.™ | Scripture quotations marked ESV are from The ESV® Bible (The Holy Bible, English Standard Version®), copyright © 2001 by Crossway, a publishing ministry of Good News Publishers. Used by permission. All rights reserved. | Scripture quotations marked NLT are taken from the Holy Bible, New Living Translation, copyright © 1996, 2004, 2015 by Tyndale House Foundation. Used by permission of Tyndale House Publishers, Inc., Carol Stream, Illinois 60188. All rights reserved.

For foreign and subsidiary rights, contact the author.

Cover design & photo by Michael B. Hardie

ISBN: 978-1-964794-64-8   1 2 3 4 5 6 7 8 9 10

Printed in the United States of America

BUILDER OF ALL THINGS

A NEW PERSPECTIVE OF PURPOSE
WITH THE
'BUSINESS PARTNER'
YOU DIDN'T KNOW YOU HAD

RICHIE BREAUX

AVAIL

WHAT'S BEING SAID ABOUT
BUILDER OF ALL THINGS

Builder of All Things is more than a book—it's a blueprint for anyone who wants to build something meaningful, whether in business, family, or faith. Richie doesn't just talk about success; he redefines it, showing that true success is found in surrender to the Master Builder. As someone who has built and scaled companies, advised leaders, and walked the road of faith-driven entrepreneurship, I can say with certainty that Richie's wisdom is the real deal. This book isn't just an inspiring read—it's a guide for those ready to build with purpose, trust, and unshakable faith.

—Dr. Rob "Dom" Douk
Founder of The Well Club
ForbesBooks author
Visionary in faith-driven leadership

To my thirteen grandchildren and beyond—my thirteen reasons for writing Builder of All Things. You are the legacy I'm building, the inspiration behind every word, and the motivation to create something that lasts. I've known the weight of hard work, the grind of making ends meet, and the highs and lows of building something from nothing. But if there's one thing I can pass down to you—not wealth, not status, not even all the lessons I've learned—it's Jesus. Nickel and dime have I none, but Jesus is the only treasure worth leaving behind. He is the foundation that never cracks, the truth that never fades, and the legacy that will outlive us all. Hold on to Him, walk in His ways, and you'll never be lost—no matter what life throws at you. With all my love, Papa.

PREFACE

The world can be tough, and I think every business owner, at some point, needs a little encouragement to keep going. The marketplace is more than just a place to work; it's also where we build, grow, and support the lives we're creating. It shapes our culture and affects so much of who we are.

I'm at a place in my career now where people—other business owners, especially those in my market—are pulling me aside or reaching out with a simple question: how did you guys do it? They want to know how we became so successful so quickly. They ask, "With everything happening in the world and in our specific market, how did you survive it? How did you grow from a small, grassroots kitchen and bath company to one of the largest residential construction companies on the island? How did you go from doing basic projects to building the most prestigious homes in Hawai'i?"

At first, I would respond with a little laugh, followed by an answer rooted in honesty: hard work, integrity, and God as my source—but I could tell they didn't really grasp the depth of what I meant. How could they? For most, it's not just words; it's the entire story, the unseen parts, the trials, and the faith it takes to walk through them.

Now, after twelve years—a span that feels symbolic, like twelve months in a year, the number of completion—I feel like I've lived a full cycle of running and operating a business. I've seen enough, fought through enough, and learned enough in this mission field to finally connect the dots for people—to go beyond the surface, answer, and show them the real source behind it all. This first book is my way of doing that. It's my introduction, my way of pulling back the curtain and sharing the truths that have been the foundation of everything we've built. This isn't just a story about success—it's a story about purpose, faith, and walking the path God laid before us.

I feel it's important to be open about my faith and who I am right from the start. For me, bringing my faith into this space feels natural and necessary. I want to be here to plant seeds of hope, purpose, and positive change in any way I can. This is what truly inspires me and makes this journey so meaningful.

This book is for all business owners and leaders, and I truly believe that, even if faith is new to you, there's something here that can bring insight and inspiration. My hope is that you'll find something meaningful to add to your journey. I know it might be easy to categorize me as "just another Christian" or think of this as a book strictly for Christians as you begin to turn the pages. But I also understand how that label can mean so many things to different people. With all the beliefs out there, it can be difficult to know what someone actually stands for. So, I like to describe my faith in a way that feels close to my heart: I'm a Jesus-centered believer.

For me, everything focuses on Jesus. I see Him as the core of my life. I believe He is the one who brings true connection and purpose. The Bible, in my view, is like a long, beautiful story with true historical accounts that highlight Jesus and reveal who He is from beginning to end. I believe He, in His role as the Son of God who came to earth and bridged the gap between us and God, offered us a way to experience deeper love, hope, and peace through a relationship with Him.

So, for me, Jesus isn't just a figure in a book; He's the true source of meaning and purpose in my life.

For in him all things were created: things in heaven and on earth, visible and invisible, whether thrones or powers or rulers or authorities; all things have been created through him and for him. He is before all things, and in Him all things hold together.
—Colossians 1:16-17

You'll notice a lot of Bible references in this book, and it's important for me to share these, as they're the foundation of how I see things. For me, the Bible is one of the greatest tools we have, right alongside my own personal connection with God. Its stories and teachings have proven to be reliable and relevant over time. So, as I share what I've learned, I'll be pulling from the Bible often; it's how I reference the truths that have been revealed to me along the way.

I'm not here to establish one doctrine over another. It's just important for me to be real with you in this book about myself and the perspective God has given me. I will speak straightforwardly about Jesus without any sugarcoating or agenda.

Let me ask you something. Wouldn't you rather I just be straight with you right from the start? They call it "B.L.U.F," bottom line up front. I want you to know exactly where I stand, where I put my faith, and where my journey has led me, rather than wrapping it all in some strategic agenda that hides the truth until the end.

I just want to be real with you, the same realness and truth I was searching for on my own journey.

This is simply my story, my experiences. Nothing hidden, nothing dressed up. I've tasted this life, and I can tell you that once I experienced Jesus, He *is* good. He is so good. And that's coming from someone who's tried so many different things in life, looking for what was real.

Over the past twelve years, I've grown in how I share Jesus's message. It's been a journey, especially in a world where faith can sometimes be misunderstood. When I first grasped what Jesus did for us, I was so excited to share this new hope with everyone. But I soon realized that, for many people, Christianity had sometimes been misused, leaving wounds. I learned how important it is to approach these conversations with sensitivity and empathy, knowing that not everyone fully understands who He is yet.

I had to learn to share Jesus's message with the service of love, patience in life, walking joy, and real integrity. This growth took time. Twelve years ago, I was known as an evangelist, excitedly shouting what He did for us. But everything changed when my wife Tiffany and I left Hawai'i for a two-week mission trip to the Philippines. Walking through the streets of Manila, seeing poverty up close, I realized that our service of love and help, while well-intentioned, wouldn't change the deeper need that remained long after we left. It struck me that while food was an act of love, people yearn for something lasting, something real. That experience changed me. I realized that true impact comes from either dedicating a lifetime to serving or sharing something that lasts. Something like the "living bread" Jesus offers. Imagine a hunger deep inside that no food can satisfy, a feeling like something is missing. I believe Jesus is the answer to that emptiness. He offers life, purpose, and meaning in a way that nothing else can.

These years in the business world have felt like a different kind of mission journey. I'm thankful for this season of growth, during which I've been able to learn, adapt, and meet people where they are with empathy—now understanding the true needs of those I serve.

So, as you step into this book, my hope is that you'll find something here that resonates, whether it's a bit of encouragement, a fresh perspective, or a reminder that you're not alone on this path. I'm not here to preach or impose but to share the truth that has shaped my life and work. I believe we all have a purpose and that, deep down, we're all looking for something real and lasting. For me, that "something" has been Jesus.

If you're open to it, let's take this journey together. I'll be honest about the lessons I've learned, the mistakes I've made, and the experiences that have changed me. Thank you for joining me. I'm grateful to share this space with you.

CONTENTS

Preface .... *ix*
Acknowledgments .... *xvii*

PART 1. BUILDING TOGETHER 21
SONG PAIRING 23
INTRODUCTION. **All Aboard** 25
CHAPTER 1. **THE SKIPPER:** *Builder of All Things* 37
CHAPTER 2. **THE SHIPMATE:** *Two Boats* 63

PART 2. BEGINNING THE COURSE ... 79
CHAPTER 3. **THE STREAM:** *Heart of a King* 81
CHAPTER 4. **THE SAIL:** *The Wind Blows* 97
CHAPTER 5. **THE SWIM:** *The 153 Season* 125

PART 3. BATTLING ADVERSITY 151
INTERLUDE. **Challenges** 153
CHAPTER 6. **THE STORM:** *Wake Him Up* 157
CHAPTER 7. **THE SNAKE:** *Air Jordan on 'Em* 181
CHAPTER 8. **THE SMOKE:** *Self-Inflicted Wounds* 201

PART 4. BIRTHING THE LEGACY ... 223
CHAPTER 9. **THE SUN:** *All Things New* 225
CHAPTER 10. **THE SCORE:** *We Already Won* 241

About the Author 261

ACKNOWLEDGMENTS

First and foremost, I give all glory to God and His son Jesus—my source of strength, grace, and wisdom. Without His presence guiding me through every season, this book wouldn't exist. He has been my foundation, my sustainer, and the architect of every opportunity, challenge, and breakthrough along the way.

To my greatest gift from God—my wife, Tiffany. You have been my rock, my iron, my unwavering partner through every high and every low. You've stood true, so true, in the system, sharpening me and positioning me to be the man, leader, and business owner God called me to be. This journey wouldn't be what it is without you walking it with me.

This book is dedicated to my legacy—starting with my four children: Takiko, Tiyarah, Jordan and Anuhea. My prayer is that you take these lessons, these principles, and multiply them. Carry them forward, refine them, and continue to build something even greater.

And to Ikaika, Kilipaki, Molly, and Ethan, thank you for the love and partnership you bring to our family. I'm blessed to witness the lives you're building together.

And to my grandchildren—Patience, Asa, Liam, Paizleigh, Mokihana, Tristany, Aurora Jean, Kaius, Maluhia, Baby Jordan, Kase, Hezekiah, and Joey—this is for you too. May you walk boldly in your calling, always knowing that what we build is never just for ourselves but for those who come after us.

To my family—Mom, Dad, Matt, Sean, and Catie—thank you for your love, support, and the foundation you laid for me.

To my Hawaiian family, who has watched me grow from a young adult to a man, your encouragement and wisdom have been invaluable.

And to all my family, friends, and classmates from Peoria, Illinois, you've been part of my story in ways big and small. Thank you for every lesson, every moment, and every memory that shaped me into the man I am today.

To my team at All Things New (ATN)—my partners, employees (past and present), and subcontractors—thank you for your loyalty, your grind, and your commitment through the ups and downs. A special shoutout to my Day Oners—David, Jeremiah, Koa, and Herbert. You've had my back since the beginning, and your belief in the vision has helped bring it to life.

A heartfelt thank you to Kiki, for helping me edit the first phase of this book. Your time and effort were instrumental in shaping these words.

To Pastor Dominic Jones, your coaching, wisdom, and guidance helped me shape the tone, direction, and impact of this book. Thank you for helping me stay true to the heart behind the message.

To Pastor Mike Kai of Inspired Church, your leadership and spiritual guidance have been a model of stewardship, faith, and purpose. Thank you for your example and the way you've poured into my journey.

To Dom Douk and the Douk family, your love, trust, and support have meant more than words can say. Thank you for allowing ATN to be part of your journey—it's been an honor.

This book is a testament to the people who have walked with me, challenged me, and believed in me. I stand on the shoulders of those who came before me, and I write for those who will come after me.

With gratitude and respect,

Richie Breaux

PART 1

BUILDING TOGETHER

SONG PAIRING

For this intro and through every chapter, I've carefully chosen a Lecrae song to pair with the words on the pages. Life has a way of giving us a soundtrack, a song that perfectly captures each season we go through. I figured, why not bring that into your reading experience? Let these songs elevate the journey, offering a deeper connection as you read. And who better than Lecrae, whose music has echoed the highs and lows of my own walk, resonating with both the struggles and the victories?

> **All Aboard Song Pairing:** "Always Knew" by Lecrae
> *All Things Work Together* (Album)[1]

You can find the playlist on Spotify by searching for "Builder of All Things" Playlist or by scanning this Spotify code.

---

[1] Lecrae, vocalist, "Always Knew," by REO and Lecrae, released September 22, 2017, track 1 on *All Things Work Together*, Reach, Columbia.

INTRODUCTION

ALL ABOARD

The Invitation to Join the Journey

> *"Come to me, all you who are weary and burdened, and I will give you rest."*
> —Matthew 11:28

Have you ever felt like you're carrying the weight of every decision, every risk, every sleepless night? Like the endless demands of running a business are just too much to handle alone? Do you sometimes wonder if anyone truly understands the pressure you face? The relentless balancing act of keeping clients happy, managing finances, and leading a team that depends on you. Do you question whether there is a greater purpose behind your endless grind—perhaps some reason that extends beyond chasing profits and performance?

What if you're not just overworked but carrying burdens that were never meant to be yours alone? As entrepreneurs, business owners, and leaders, we often take on more than others realize. It's like everyone around us is lifting a manageable weight while we're left struggling to bear something far heavier. It feels like being in a gym where everyone else is lifting one hundred pounds while we're struggling with 450. The responsibilities of clients, employees, products, finances, and health just keep piling on until the burden feels impossible to carry any longer.

Have you asked yourself, even in those moments when you hit your goals, whether the success you're working so hard for will really bring fulfillment? We're constantly chasing after success, but the challenges of keeping the doors open never let up. What if, instead of running harder, there was someone who could walk this journey with us, offering a source of strength, guidance, and purpose far beyond what we can find on our own?

The challenges are constant, and sometimes, they keep us up at night, leaving us unable to sleep because no matter where we go, we carry it all with us. We're driven by this hunger for success, chasing it relentlessly. But along the way, we face challenge after challenge: paying taxes, managing payroll, chasing invoices, and trying to keep everything afloat. It's overwhelming. Sometimes, we get caught in a whirlwind of survival, scrambling for resources like bank loans and investors as we max out our credit cards. All just to make it over the next hurdle. We search for the right connections, scroll through social media for inspiration, listen to speakers, follow quotes, hire business coaches—anything to feel like we're moving in the right direction.

But what if there's another kind of resource? A source of guidance more powerful than all the coaches, consultants, and motivational quotes combined? Something you could tap into, not just to realign your path, but to walk it with confidence, even through the darkest moments? Imagine a journey where every step you take is guided by an unseen hand, a partner who knows the paths you've missed, the challenges you face, and the dreams you hold deep within.

We've all had those sleepless nights, lying awake, staring at the ceiling, wondering if we're making the right decision, unsure which road to take. But what if there was a way to know for sure? What if there was a source of light to illuminate the path designed specifically for you, one that not only shows you the way but also fills you with confidence and clarity about where you're going and why?

After years of navigating the demands of building a business, juggling endless responsibilities, and facing moments that left us questioning everything, my wife Tiffany and I realized that there was more to this journey than simply pushing forward. We found ourselves reaching for something greater. A source of understanding our purpose that changed the trajectory of not only our business but also our lives.

I can't tell you how deeply grateful I am to open up this part of my life and share our story with those who may be feeling the same weight. I know what it's like to chase your passions relentlessly, pouring everything you have into your business, only to feel burnt out and exhausted, wondering if it's worth it. I've been there, feeling like it's all on me, shouldering a burden that only seemed to grow heavier. But one day, everything changed.

As I share my personal experiences, I strongly feel that Tiffany and I are collaborating on this. This book stems from our shared experiences in building our business. When Tiffany and I launched our first business, I personally had no clue what I was doing or getting into. It took a lot of studying and going through the process to adapt and grow.

OUR BACKGROUND

After enduring overwhelming hardships, like two devastating house fires in my childhood and Tiffany's family struggling with homelessness during her high school years, we began our life together from a place of no financial support. The idea of starting a business felt like an impossible dream, weighed down by our lack of resources. Yet, we pushed forward, leaning on nothing but faith, refusing to give up even when everything seemed stacked against us. We started from scratch together and persevered.

We have faced many ups and downs, drawing strength from our previous life experiences. Even in our toughest moments, we found that these experiences brought us closer to each other. Over twelve years of running the business, we have built and now steward an award-winning, nationally recognized, eight-figure business.

Like many of you reading this book, I faced my fair share of challenges growing up. But looking back, I can see how my purpose unfolded. My family did not have a lot of money and lacked the means to help me financially beyond high school.

My parents sat me down and, with heavy hearts, told me that they were still struggling to recover from the devastation of our most recent house fire. As difficult as it was to hear, they reminded me of my gift as an athlete and how I could use that gift to earn scholarships and fund my education.

Their words filled me with determination and a sense of purpose, inspiring the hustle within me. From my young perspective, sports scholarships felt like my only lifeline to a college education. It was the only path I could see then, the one glimmer of hope in a future that otherwise felt uncertain and out of reach.

The dream came true when I was recruited to Lake Forest College to play football, with everything paid for. But after just one semester, that dream slipped through my fingers. I lost it all because of a low GPA, overwhelmed by the load of being a full-time football player while juggling six demanding classes during my freshman fall semester. Without the guidance I desperately needed, I couldn't keep up. Losing that opportunity left me facing impossible tuition fees and feeling lost and vulnerable.

I was then recruited into the Navy with what I felt was the last option I had to make a difference in my life. Talk about a difficult pill to swallow at nineteen years old. After I completed boot camp, my first duty station was Pearl Harbor, where I immediately met Tiffany. I felt like I went from rock bottom to hitting the jackpot in the year 2000 with the opportunity to move from my little city of Peoria, Illinois, to Hawai'i.

Now, after twenty-four years with Tiffany, shaped by a deep love and guided by something bigger than ourselves, we're finally bringing this book to life. We're excited to share our story, the journey of building a business, and the impact that the special guidance of our faith has had every step along the way.

WHAT TO EXPECT IN THIS BOOK

The main takeaway I hope you find in this book is the power of a fresh perspective to ignite and navigate your unique calling. I believe each of us has something important to steward, whether it's a business, a family, a vision, or a community. Stewardship isn't just about managing and caring for what we have; it's also about leading with purpose, using our resources wisely, and creating something that serves others and lasts.

Whatever you're working on—whether you're building a business, nurturing your own home, or leading a team—it's more than just the success of fulfilling a vision. It's also about building something meaningful. In this book, I also hope to spark a deeper calling in you, encouraging you to view your journey through a lens of purpose and significance. This perspective is what brings a lasting impact that goes beyond financial gain or outward success, anchoring you in something that leaves a legacy.

Many of us step into entrepreneurship driven by a desire for financial freedom. But it's your perspective that shapes the real rewards of the journey as you decide whether what you build will stand the test of time and serve people. If you picked up this book hoping for a quick roadmap to more profit or a fast track to financial success, let me be real with you. This might lose your interest pretty quickly. But I'm asking, no—I'm pleading with you—to stick with it anyway.

I do believe that what you'll gain here is worth far more than a balance sheet can show.

Looking back, I can see how my path was meant for entrepreneurship, and the lessons I've learned are universal. Whether you're launching a new business, running a nonprofit, or already in the thick of things, maintaining the right perspective is what keeps you grounded, giving you endurance, purpose, and even peace when challenges come.

Maybe you're starting a business to follow a passion, create generational wealth, or make a lasting impact. Whatever your reasons, the insights in this book are here to help you see it through.

One of my top five favorite movies of all time is *The Family Man*, starring Nicholas Cage as Jack. If you haven't seen it, it's about this guy named Jack whose fast-paced luxury lifestyle changes on a Christmas night when he stumbles into a grocery store holdup and makes a deal with the gunman. Like a modern retelling of *A Christmas Carol*,[2] the next morning, Jack wakes up in bed next to his college love on Christmas morning, whom he left years ago to pursue his successful career. He's shocked to discover his former life no longer exists and finds himself living through this alternate universe and perspective, where he must choose between rebuilding his prior successful lifestyle or sticking with what he believes is the toned-down version with the woman he once loved and two kids.

Jack's sudden shift in reality enables him to dig deep and see what truly matters to him. He sees his life from a new

---

[2] Robert Zemeckis, *A Christmas Carol* (November 6, 2009; Burbank, CA: Walt Disney Studios).

perspective, appreciating the importance of family over material success.[3] The contrast between his two lives emphasizes the impact of perspective.

As author John Martin describes in his book *Choose Your Perspective*, **perspective** is the way you see life, and **perception** is understanding what you see.[4] My goal in this book is to go even further and help you develop a vision that brings ***purpose and power*** to your life.

If we understand the power of renewing our perspective in our everyday lives, we can potentially change how we perceive our circumstances. Being open to new ways of seeing things can lead to a shift in our perception and develop a new way of believing what we see. Being more aware of our path and willing to see things in a positive light can alter our viewpoints, potentially leading to personal growth and even healing. This can help clear the fog from our lens, so we can see our purpose in life with clarity, positioning us to reclaim our belief, stand in our truth, and walk confidently in our power.

So, what if I told you that I have a new perspective that ties everything together and a fundamental truth that can transform your life and how you perceive your calling and life forever? Are you interested?

While I'm eager to share, it does make Tiffany and me quite vulnerable. Being transparent about our business and life events exposes us to sharing deeper, real-time events that have occurred. We have many more books to come after this one that we are eager to write that focus on applications in

---

3 Brett Ratner, *The Family Man* (December 22, 2000; Universal City, CA: Universal Pictures).
4 John Martin, *Choose Your Perspective* (Shippensburg, PA: Sound Wisdom, 2019).

business and leadership in the marketplace. Still, this book serves as the most important stepping stone, the foundation—its contents are crucial. It's a must-read.

This first book is designed to lay the foundation for stepping into your calling in life. Whether you are beginning your journey in entrepreneurship, in the midst of running a business, or facing difficulties in your company, this book is for you. We've also experienced the overwhelming highs and lows that come with running a business. Very few like to talk about the hardships.

As business owners, we rarely get the chance to lower our guard and reveal what's really happening behind the scenes. We constantly have to project confidence, always wearing the face that sells our products and services. Just one hint of the struggles or challenges we're facing can feel risky. It might mean losing future opportunities that only add to our burdens when, sometimes, all we really need is just a few more clients to make things right.

Perhaps you've faced declining sales and skyrocketing overheads or the IRS scrutinizing your taxes. Maybe cash flow is dropping, and you're struggling to keep up with payments. Maybe your staff are either not showing up or not working at full capacity, leading to a high turnover rate. Competitors might be luring away clients, resulting in dissatisfied customers and potential legal action. The changing market landscape could be prompting you to adapt your services or products where it feels like you're consumed by busyness, constantly chasing after cash and unpaid invoices. Or the catch twenty-two: your family life is slowly slipping away due to your overwhelming involvement needed to keep the business afloat, but if you take a step back, even for a day, you fear the company could collapse. We have seen and experienced all these common challenges in entrepreneurship. We want to assure you that this book offers guidance to keep your business afloat even in the face of adversity.

NAVIGATING THIS BOOK

In Part 1: Building Together, we will explore how shifting your perspective to see yourself as a steward rather than an owner can unlock a source of strength and enable you to guide your business with purpose—not just for profit. At the end of chapter 1, we will do something a little different—I suggest that instead of going straight on to chapter 2, you jump ahead to the end of the book for a sneak preview of chapter 10 before circling back to chapter 2. This is crucial for understanding my perspective, and rather than spoiling the end, I believe this will enhance your journey through the book.

In Part 2: Beginning the Course, we lay the foundations for shifting your drive from ambition to calling and aligning your heart with your purpose, which will set you up to stay on course throughout the inevitable storms that occur in the life of any business.

In Part 3: Battling Adversity, we will look at the different kinds of challenges you can face, how to identify them, and the best approach to overcoming these, both practically and spiritually.

Finally, in Part 4: Birthing the Legacy, we will look at how seeing the bigger picture can enable you to lead with confidence, be more creative in problem-solving, and waste less energy on things you cannot fix. Ultimately, I hope you will realize how empowering it can be when you embrace the belief that our paths are predetermined.

Thank you again for taking the time to learn from our experiences and reflections on faith and business. In this book, we hope our shared path can provide a solid foundation for your business journey, ensuring you sail through rough seas and emerge stronger.

Welcome aboard!

Richie and Tiffany

CHAPTER 1

THE SKIPPER:
Builder of All Things

Stewardship vs Ownership

"For every house is built by someone, but
the builder of all things is God."
—Hebrews 3:4 (ESV)

GRAND ARTIST

I'll do my best to bring this to life for you. As a builder, I genuinely appreciate every moment each day. During my morning drives up the H1 East highway, I usually try to ease into the day with a steaming cup of hazelnut-flavored Lion coffee while in my work truck, tiptoeing through the usual traffic. As I'm headed to one of our construction sites, these moments behind the wheel offer more than just a drive to work and some really good local coffee; they're a chance for me to savor the island's stunning scenery.

I've always loved looking up at the Hawaiian mountains as they provide a majestic backdrop against the slow traffic. In the Midwest of Peoria, Illinois, where I was born and raised, the landscape was characterized by flat lands and cornfields. In Hawai'i, on the other hand, lush green mountains cover almost every drive, regardless of which side of the island you're on. As a construction company owner, this view has always inspired me. A big part of the appreciation I feel when I gaze at the beauty of these mountains is that man didn't make them. The sun rises behind them, washing the sky with color and light like a picture painted by a **Grand Artist**.

Looking at mountains always fills me with a sense of awe. It's so humbling. It truly minimizes all I think I have accomplished in my life. I often contemplate the luxury homes our amazing team is working on and think about how those big houses seem so tiny in comparison. I recall a specific moment involving one of our projects in prime Orange County, California. This property was positioned at the end of a cul-de-sac at the summit of the Newport coast, offering sick (amazingly good, outstanding) views. After a long, very challenging day of work on this house, I remember a specific evening driving down the mountain back to my hotel. It was a day I felt defeated, as I was in new territory outside of Hawai'i and couldn't seem to get the traction to move things forward like I was used to. But what really challenged me was the fact that I was alone. I was away from my wife, Tiffany, and our family for a week at a time for months.

NOTHING CHANGED EXCEPT HOW I LOOKED AT IT. MY PERCEPTION WAS REDEFINED.

As I drove down and looked up at the house, still strategizing my game plan for the rest of the week, an unexpected revelation struck me. Two things became increasingly apparent. First, the grandeur of the mountain became more evident—from below, I was able to see how grand it actually was. Second, the house gradually shrank until it was only a mere speck. All the houses on the hill looked like a bag of Skittles scattered across a golf course, ultimately overshadowed by this majestic creation. This experience and moment opened my eyes to the power of perspective in how we perceive the world as individuals and how we should respectfully position ourselves. Standing at the foot of this grand mountain made me realize how small my daily problems, challenges, and struggles were in comparison to its size. The house we were remodeling had felt so significant when we were on top of the mountain, along with the pressure of the natural construction stress it brought me that day. Now, it was so small that all I could do was laugh. Nothing changed except how I looked at it. My perception was redefined.

As a business owner and builder of custom homes, I know the intricate process it takes to bring a structure to life. The scheduling, the design, the blueprints, each nail meticulously placed, every piece working together for structural strength and functionality. Everything is thoughtfully engineered to not only stand strong but also create a space where life will be lived and loved.

Now, imagine standing in front of a towering skyscraper. If I asked you whether human hands crafted it or it somehow just appeared, it would seem ridiculous to think it simply exists without a builder or design. As a builder myself, I can't overlook the logic of creation. And when I look at our vast, perfectly balanced world, with the oceans, the seasons, the towering mountains, the sustainability of life and resources, and the Earth's perfect placement in the universe from the sun, it's clear to me there must be a Creator—a Master Architect, a CEO, an Owner, an ultimate Builder of All Things. To deny that would be to ignore the very essence of what I understand so deeply in my own work and business.

This perspective brought me a deep sense of peace, knowing that this Creator oversees everything. It revealed to me the profound impact that shifting my focus could have—not only on my understanding of life but on how I view my circumstances. Now, when I think of the mountains, they pull me into a place of reverence. They're a reminder that we're part of something far greater, a vast creation that God Himself crafted.

Every day, this perspective helps me to align my heart, reminding me who I truly serve and who the real Owner of everything is. I am not the owner; I'm simply a steward. Knowing this has freed me. It repositions my role—not as the one in control, but as someone entrusted with a purpose, serving the One who built it all.

THE SPOTTER

As I share our company stories and our humble beginnings, I'm thankful that God positioned our hearts from the very beginning to steward the vision He had of our business. By sharing this, I hope you will understand the importance of including God from the very beginning.

To be honest, we had no idea what we were getting ourselves into. Not a clue! All we knew for certain was that we had God with us. This time in our lives aligned with a season of deep faith for Tiffany and me, knowing if we did start a business, it would honor God. As the years went by, I realized that I had no guidelines for incorporating my faith and beliefs into the business, let alone starting or running one. I was just ready to climb this mountain with God.

Growing up, I was an ambitious young kid, constantly exploring the unknown. My mom used to share with me how I would always just run off and do dangerous things. One of my favorite "dangerous things" to do was to climb. It was quite common for me to climb walls that a kid my age had no business climbing, and I would do it with absolute fearlessness. My parents had a difficult time keeping up with me; I'd take off the moment I felt that first taste of freedom. I just couldn't be held back! Here are a few memories worth sharing. I remember going with my mom to the bank when I was around four years old. While my mom was cashing a check, the bank teller directed her to turn around as I climbed the bank's structural rock column all the way to the ceiling. I was at a point where I was stuck and needed help. My mom was just tall enough to grab me and help me down.

There was also another scary moment when I was with my dad and family while he was rock climbing a one-hundred-foot rock wall. He did this as a hobby during my childhood days. He would have gear strapped on for safety and climb regularly with his friends. Unknowingly to my dad and family, I followed him from behind with no gear. If I were to guess, I would say I was about six years old. I was following my dad's path and had my eyes fully on him. I stayed focused on what was in front of me and kept looking up to grab the next bulging rock edges to keep my pace, and I got pretty darn far. Imagine the feeling of the rough texture of the rock beneath your fingertips and the sense of excitement as you look up.

As I climbed higher, the view around me became more breathtaking, and I slowly felt the freedom of what my dad experienced when he climbed. Eventually, I realized there was nowhere else to go; the next rock to grab was too far out of reach for a six-year-old kid, so, as you can imagine, fear kicked in. I finally looked down, began to panic, and started to cry. My perspective instantly and dramatically changed. When my dad discovered me, he immediately headed toward me and was able to climb over and, thankfully, save me.

Later in my childhood, in an alley behind my parents' house, I climbed a tree to a very high point like a fearless expert to hide from some neighborhood kids while playing. A kid named Scott finally found me hiding up there as part of some outdoor game we had created. Out of excitement, he started to throw branches and things at me to get me to climb down, eventually causing me to fall for the first time in my climbing career. This fall was unlike any fall I had experienced. I actually felt like I was floating on the way down. I hit the ground hard enough to knock me unconscious and break my arm, putting me into a cast for months.

> **LIKE A MUSCLE, FAITH CAN GET STRONGER AND STRONGER, OR IT CAN POTENTIALLY GET INJURED IF WE ARE NOT IN THE PRESENCE OF A SPOTTER.**

Only then did I realize the risks involved in my fearless climbing attempts. After that, I stopped climbing just for the sake of it. I allowed the injury to paralyze me for a while, fearing to climb with the same courage. It took me years to rebuild my confidence and climb again. As a builder, I need to use ladders, lifts, and climb scaffolding, all essential for constructing homes. So, I had to face my fears and overcome them.

I learned something about myself: my bold climbing escapades as a young child began with the presence of my parents. Slowly along the way, they instilled confidence in me that I would be saved even to the point of climbing halfway up a one-hundred-foot wall. This confidence became ingrained in me, leading me to attempt climbs even when my parents were not around to save me if I got into trouble and badly injured myself.

Looking back now, this reminds me of how our faith is. Like a muscle, it can get stronger and stronger, or it can potentially get injured if we are not in the presence of a spotter. In weightlifting, a spotter is someone who assists the lifter during their exercise, primarily to ensure safety. The spotter's role is to help the lifter complete their reps, especially when they're pushing heavy weights or nearing muscle fatigue. In terms of faith, a spotter could be a trusted spiritual guide, a community, or even God Himself. Someone or something that helps us build resilience and endurance in our faith journey, catching us if we falter and encouraging us to keep growing safely and steadily.

When God is with us, there are moments when He reaches down, takes hold of the lifting bar, and guides us with His strength. And then there are times when He lets us bear the weight on our own, yet He's always there, right beside us, ready to catch us if we stumble. He wants us to grow in confidence—not in our own strength but in His. Just like those moments when I was climbing, it's a powerful reminder that stepping out in faith means leaning on God, not relying on my own strength.

There's a story in the Bible about a fisherman named Peter who was a close follower of Jesus. One night, Peter and the other disciples saw Jesus walking on water toward them during a storm. Peter was amazed and wanted to join Him, but walking on water was beyond anything he could imagine doing on his own. With Jesus encouraging him, Peter took that first step out of the boat. It was a bold act of faith that would shape him in ways he couldn't yet see. And Peter actually walked on water, stepping forward and toward Jesus. His courage to do this didn't come from his own strength; it came from the fact that Jesus was right there with him. That physical presence gave him the confidence to do something extraordinary.

Later, when Jesus was no longer physically with Peter, Peter didn't lose that courage. Instead, he grew even bolder because Jesus had promised something remarkable: God's presence would remain with him—not beside him but within him—through His Spirit. Having His Spirit within is like having a "spotter" within. Someone who provides you with confidence and courage. And it's not limited to a specific place or moment. The Spotter is always there, empowering and reminding us of what we're capable of when we trust and lean into that connection.

Later, this same fisherman, who had once hesitated and feared the unknown, found himself boldly standing in front of thousands, confidently sharing the message of Jesus's resurrection. Imagine that—going from casting nets to delivering what was basically a TED Talk to a massive crowd. But here's the thing: Peter only dared to step out onto the water in the first place because he had Jesus—his ultimate "Spotter"—right there with him, ready to catch him if he fell. That same presence is what gave him the confidence to speak with boldness later on.

It's scary to think about the reality of climbing the one-hundred-foot wall without gear now, knowing in the real world, I could have died if I'd fallen. With God, He will not let you fall if He is present, especially if it's the wall He is guiding or commanding you to climb.

I believe we all have stories where God has saved us or intervened to steer us away from poor decisions, particularly when we are in His presence. But what if He is calling you to climb a mountain? Imagine being called to face a moment that seems far too big, a challenge that feels like a mountain towering over you, daring you to climb it. For most of us, fear takes over, and we start to believe we're incapable.

Take these biblical figures, for example. As an adult, Moses was a man who had distanced himself from his past in Egypt, living a quiet life as a shepherd, far from the hardships and struggles of his people. Then, one day, he felt a calling, a pull he couldn't ignore. He was called to climb his own mountain—a call from the "Spotter" to return to the very place he had once fled. His mission was to stand before the mighty Pharaoh, the ruler of Egypt, and demand freedom for an entire nation. Imagine the weight of that responsibility. Moses wasn't a powerful speaker. He actually doubted his abilities and questioned why he was chosen. Yet, despite his fears, he stepped forward like Peter, placing one foot in front of the other. Forward and toward his destiny, knowing that he wasn't climbing this mountain alone.

Then there's Joseph. He was a young man who had been betrayed by his own brothers, sold into slavery, and wrongfully imprisoned. For years, he endured hardship after hardship, separated from his family and his dreams. But one day, he was called by the "Spotter" to stand before Pharaoh himself to interpret a mysterious dream that no one else could explain. Imagine Joseph's nerves as he stood before the most powerful ruler of his time, as if facing a mountain, knowing that his life could change in an instant, either for better or for worse. He had no guarantee of success, no certainty of what the future held. Yet he took a step forward and toward his destiny, speaking with courage and trusting that he was meant to be there and that all he had endured had led him to this moment.

And then there's David, a young shepherd boy with no armor and no experience in battle yet called by the "Spotter" to face a giant. Goliath was massive, a warrior who made everyone around him tremble. But David, armed with nothing but a sling and a few stones, looked up at this mountain of a man and somehow found the courage to stand his ground. He didn't have the strength or the skill to match Goliath, but what he did have was a quiet confidence, a faith that he wasn't truly facing the giant alone. Then he stepped forward and toward his destiny. With a single stone, he defeated the one who seemed undefeatable.

Each of these people stood at the base of a mountain they never expected to climb. A calling that seemed beyond their strength. Yet, they found the courage to take that first step forward and toward their calling to face their fears and embrace their purpose. Their stories remind us that even in our most intimidating moments, when the path ahead looks impossible, we're never truly climbing alone. There's a strength available to us, a guiding presence that can lead us through the challenges we fear the most and help us overcome obstacles we never imagined we could face.

I've spoken with so many people who felt the pull toward something greater but hesitated, fearing they didn't have the "right gear" to begin their climb. They held back, convinced they weren't equipped for the journey, and in doing so, missed the incredible path of growth, trust, and the relationship that comes from stepping out in faith.

But look at Moses. All he had was a simple shepherd's rod, a worn-down ordinary stick. It wasn't a weapon; it wasn't powerful in itself, but it became the tool that parted seas and delivered a nation. Then there's Joseph, who was given nothing more than a dream—just one vision, a flicker of hope in the darkest of times—and he held onto it through betrayal, prison, and years of waiting, trusting that somehow it would guide him to his purpose. And David, a young shepherd boy, who faced a giant with nothing but a rock in his hand—no armor, no sword, just a stone and his courage—yet it was all he needed to conquer what seemed impossible.

Each of these heroes started with what looked like nothing, but they took what they had and trusted that it was enough. They didn't wait for the perfect moment or the perfect resources; they leaned into what was given to them and watched as it became exactly what they needed. Their journeys show us that we don't need every answer or all the right "gear" to step into our calling. Sometimes, all it takes is faith to pick up what's in our hands and trust that the One who calls us will also equip us, guiding us to places we could never reach on our own.

HE IS ALWAYS WORKING FOR YOU IF YOU LET HIM.

When we started our business, we could barely handle small kitchen and bath renovations, maybe ten to fifteen projects a year. Back then, I never could have imagined where we are now. But by stepping out in faith, year after year, here we are—building multimillion-dollar custom homes. It's a reminder that growth is a process we all have to go through, and along the way, you need a spotter. Sometimes, that "Spotter" shows up in ways you least expect. He shows up through prayer, through people that He places in your path, and through doors He opens that you didn't even know were there. He is always working for you if you let Him.

When you're given a calling, a vision uniquely meant for you, God often hands you just enough to get started—what I call "minimal gear." It's rarely the fully stocked toolkit we might hope for. Instead, it's a bare-bones set of essentials, just enough to take that first step, and here is why: so that we're drawn to lean on Him, not on our own resources. He wants us to look up, not around, for the support we need as we face the challenges ahead.

When I first stepped out into my calling and launched the business with Tiffany, all I really had was an enduring, childlike faith, the bare minimum of resources, and a belief that, if trouble came, He would step in, just as my dad had always done for me growing up. There was no safety net, no grand blueprint, no perfect plan. I knew I was headed toward something bigger than myself.

But in those moments of uncertainty, I felt that God Himself became our gear, our strength, our guidance, and our protection. He filled the gaps, provided direction, and gave us the courage to keep going. So, that's exactly what we did. With minimal gear but a heart full of trust, we took that first step and began our climb, learning along the way that every small bit we were given was just enough for the moment. It wasn't about what we lacked; it was about the One who walked beside us, supplying what we needed each step of the way.

> *"I lift up my eyes to the mountains—where does my help come from? My help comes from the LORD, the Maker of heaven and earth."*
> —Psalms 121:1-2

ALL THINGS NEW

Just before we started our business, we were just getting by, living in a low-income area on the west side of Oahu. Barely making enough to pay the essential bills and living off food stamps, I found myself in survival mode after being laid off from my previous job due to lack of work. I was calling and looking for every side job I could find. I hadn't even considered starting a business.

I was able to gain traction and find some small projects, continuing to take advantage of various small opportunities that came my way. At that time, I didn't even realize the level of skill and quality God had instilled in me as a builder or renovator. Though I had my Navy administration experience and journeyman carpenter license from a four-year trade school, I had not fully realized the extent of my capabilities and skills yet.

I remember the time when the idea of launching our own business really started for me. I was in grind mode and in a season of serving my community with my carpentry craft, leaving every door open for more work and hustling to the best of my ability. The moment unfolded when I received a personal call from someone at our church in Hawai'i, asking me to help his local friend in need.

This friend was a respected local firefighter with a family who happened to be in a tough situation that could have resulted in the loss of his home. The friend had hired a local contractor who took a significant down payment of about $70,000, did some initial demo work valued at around $10,000 to $15,000, and then disappeared, leaving the homeowner with little money and an unfinished house. They were losing cash fast with absolutely no movement on the construction of their home.

The gravity of this situation left me feeling burdened and deeply saddened for his family. As I contemplated the challenges that lay ahead of them, I struggled to fathom how someone could perpetrate such a scam and then walk away with such a large sum of money without facing any consequences. The company in question had used a false name and license and could not be located. I felt led to help this man and his family in any way I could. I wanted to leverage my connections and experience with tradesmen and inspectors, drawing on my trade skills to make the place livable for them. I hoped to ease their burden during this challenging time and make it a little easier for them to move in. I didn't charge anything.

This experience really weighed on my heart and inspired me to serve the people of Oahu, protecting homeowners from scams like that. As I looked into it more and talked with locals, I started to see a tough reality. A common problem that everyone felt. It wasn't just a small issue; it was something bigger, something even the city leaders couldn't fully handle. Families in the area were raising kids in homes that were falling apart, needing basic repairs to make them safe and healthy or give them more room to build as their families grew.

This insight motivated me to demonstrate my faith and integrate God into my craft, especially since I wasn't seeing it in the local construction market. I wanted to bring something new to the forefront. The bottom line was that I felt called by God.

As I shared my desire, burden, and vision with Tiffany, we decided to give it more thought and prayer. Launching a business to support our family, with four children aged seven to sixteen at the time, was unrealistic, considering we had no financial savings, no family with a healthy financial background, and no prior business experience. It was extremely frightening. It felt like God was calling us to climb a huge rock mountain wall with absolutely no gear, but we had a vision.

When I was laid off, Tiffany and I devoted ourselves to building our relationship with God and serving our local church, Hope Chapel West Oahu (now known as Inspire Church), under the leadership of Senior Pastor Mike Kai. At that time, my relationship with God was vibrant and passionate. I felt like an evangelist, eagerly sharing my faith through music and any other available opportunity presented to me.

During this season, something on the earth shifted, and God started making His move. It was like He knew we had started climbing, and He began providing us with the gear we needed to make our way up.

I got an unexpected call from a colleague of Tiffany's who shared that God had prompted him to bless me with some carpentry tools. It was an offer I couldn't refuse, and I happily accepted. He instructed me to go to a warehouse in Waipahu, Hawai'i, to collect the tools, as he was venturing into photography and no longer needed them due to a prior back injury.

When I arrived at the warehouse in my small green Ford Ranger truck, he greeted me and guided me into his father-in-law's warehouse, a space filled with towering shelves stocked with various construction tools and equipment. The racks towered three stories high, filled with numerous skill saws, chop saws, nail guns, cement mixers, etc. It was a profoundly moving experience for me, and I was overwhelmed by his generosity. I teared up in disbelief, but in a moment of wonderment, I whispered to God, "What are you doing? What in the heck am I going to do with these? I can't even store them!"

Tiffany's colleague looked at me with a smirk on his face and said, "You're going to need a bigger truck."

I eventually figured out how to transport and store the tools in three different locations. I didn't know what to do with such a huge collection. This unexpected turn of events and my newfound tools marked the beginning of my journey to assist others in need. I felt as if God had personally provided me with the minimal gear.

I remember reaching out to my church, excited to offer any carpentry help I could. Although they could only think of small tasks at the time, I felt that God's call was preparing me for something greater.

In November 2011, I finally received a call to return to my previous company after being unemployed for just over a year. I had been with them for six years prior, and they were beginning to pick up more jobs again. The timing of this call, combined with everything else going on, was in sync with all that God was starting to reveal. We were at a crossroads, deciding which direction to take—return to my consistent forty-hour-a-week job or kickstart the business we felt God was leading us to build.

My previous company asked if I could return in a few months, but I told them I needed time to consider. They offered me the first job opportunity but were clear that they would need to offer it to someone else if I declined when they called again. After discussing it with Tiffany, she suggested that returning to the old forty-hour-a-week job might be safer. There were no guarantees we could run our own business in the construction market, which was entirely new territory for us.

As a wife and mother of four kids, Tiffany showed incredible courage by having faith and praying with me as we considered starting this construction venture. While I could have pursued another carpentry job, being part of the carpenters' union limited my options, and I didn't want to face the uncertainty of being on the union bench if things didn't work out. It was challenging, but we leaned on God's wisdom, prayed, and utilized our discernment to determine our next move.

Fortunately, during my season of unemployment, Tiffany had gained some confidence in our capabilities. I had experience working with my wife and kids on remodeling her brother's house. The kids were involved in tasks like handling drywall, painting, and installing flooring and cabinets. We collaborated to help my brother-in-law settle into his new place during my off-season, allowing my family to witness firsthand what we were capable of. While this provided them with an understanding of my abilities, we were still unsure whether we could handle the business aspect.

Having this foundational experience in mind and pondering the call to return to my previous company, I sought guidance from God. I asked for a clear and unmistakable confirmation from God so that my wife and I would feel confident that this decision was from Him. We prayed and fasted together, longing for a supernatural sign or a crystal-clear confirmation that we were on the right path.

The days passed, months came and went, and finally, that day arrived—the phone rang. It was my former foreman calling to see if I wished to return. I looked at my wife, and she looked at me. We realized we hadn't received the crystal-clear confirmation we'd prayed for, so I decided right there to accept the forty-hour-a-week carpenter job to provide for my family, as I believed that's where I needed to be. God had given no other sign.

But my foreman's unexpected words took me aback. Despite his almost decade-long tenure with the company, he sternly advised me against returning. He explained that the job offer would only last a short time, and I would likely be sidelined and benched for a significant duration. In a union setting, being benched typically means that when there's no work available, you're placed on a waiting list until new work assignments come up. In other words, after this temporary job ended, I would likely endure a period without work before I'd be called again for another assignment.

He conveyed that the work involved tasks outside the realm of a carpenter's role, with a significant portion being subcontractor work stretching over a year and a half without any promises of future employment. He urged me not to return for my own sake and that of my family. He explained that he had already lost the battle to keep the carpentry work in-house, as opposed to subcontracting it all out, while trying to advocate for the carpenters within the company. As a result, he had decided to quit.

After ending the call, I turned to my wife and shared the unexpected turn of events. At that moment, we both realized that this wasn't the path we were meant to take. That marked the beginning of our journey to launch our own company: All

Things New. Credit goes to Tiffany, who received the name from God. The name deeply resonated with us, reflecting our faith and the transformative work we believe God has done—and will continue to do—not only in our lives but also in the lives of those we are called to serve.

All Things New reflects how God has prepared us to serve all people, equipping us to build and renovate all aspects of construction while introducing a new way of doing business in our market.

I wanted to share this foundational story to emphasize the desires and aspirations that drive us when we consider starting a business or stepping into our calling. Often, there's an eagerness to push forward without God, trying to climb the walls in front of us on our own. But it's crucial to pause and recognize the lessons we've learned along the way as they prepare us for what's ahead.

Stepping out in faith to start a business is a bold move, and the first essential step is ensuring you're climbing the right wall—moving in the direction aligned with your purpose.

THE MASTER BUILDER

In the construction industry, intricate sequences must be respected among multiple trades. For instance, it would be disastrous to have a painter working on the ceiling on the same day the flooring is installed. There's a specific order that must be followed to ensure the quality and efficiency of the work. We witness this need for a specific order and flow in various aspects of life, including understanding God's plans and calling in our lives.

When my wife and I embarked on the journey of launching our business, we understood the importance of positioning ourselves before God first, acknowledging that He is the **Master Builder** and the ultimate Builder of All Things—even of our business. By positioning ourselves as stewards rather than mere owners, we chose to trust and not force our way into building a business without Him. We believed God had guided us and confirmed it in our hearts. We needed to start with a foundation of prayer and confirmation. We knew that the rock wall in front of us was His wall, and whenever we got stuck along the way up, He would immediately save us. We now knew we were on the right path, and even if we took a wrong turn, He would guide us back.

If I take the wings of the morning
and dwell in the uttermost parts of the sea,
even there your hand shall lead me,
and your right hand shall hold me.
—*Psalms 139:9-10 (ESV)*

Some entrepreneurs, including us, start each day with a fire inside, ready to take off and make bold moves that push them right to the edge of their limits; it's that relentless drive—the kind that doesn't quit no matter how tough the road gets. We all carry a "Shoe Dog" determination, like Phil Knight, the founder of Nike, who started with nothing but a dream, selling shoes out of the trunk of his car. He hustled, faced rejection, and overcame countless setbacks, fueled by a vision he refused to give up on. But even with that Shoe Dog mentality—with the energy and determination to push forward—we need a spotter in our lives, someone to guide us, catch us when the weight gets too heavy, and keep us grounded when we're tempted to go off course.

Our spotter is no ordinary helper; He is the Master Builder Himself. He's the One who designed the blueprint of our lives and sees the big picture when all we see are the pieces. Even if we find ourselves far off course and almost out of bounds, we can trust that His guidance will be our solid constant and know that He has us. As entrepreneurs, the idea of His guidance can sound abstract or even fuzzy. But for us, the role of the Builder of All Things has been anything but vague. He's been the anchor, the "clutch" factor, in specific, tangible ways. He shows up exactly when we need Him most, often in ways we don't expect. When the pressure is on, when we're out of options or strength, He delivers what we need, whether it's peace, guidance, provision, or even a miracle. He reminds us that He's always in control, even in our most critical moments.

For us, this guidance hasn't just been about a warm feeling. It's been about Him showing up in concrete, undeniable ways, ways that opened doors to specific projects, brought the right people onto our team, and protected us from projects that could have brought hardships, even when we couldn't see the whole picture at the time. These are the moments that remind us why we trust Him with our business.

This decision to start the company allowed us the opportunity to responsibly manage the ownership of this business God entrusted to us. In hindsight, waiting for a few months, praying, and trusting we could rely on Him set the perfect tone for our new endeavor. It provided us with a steadfast position regardless of the inevitable challenges and uncertainties that would come our way. I encourage readers to seek, ask, and trust in the answers they receive, recognizing that there is a God who is ultimately in control and the true Builder of All Things. Even if you stray from trusting Him, there's always an opportunity to realign and make amends.

Over the next decade, my wife and I embarked on a journey to figure this out with His guidance. Through this experience, I can now share this journey with you. This book starts from the beginning when I had no playbook or tangible guidance and how that helped me recognize His greatness despite my limitations.

We all work on building things, but at the same time, we are like the houses being built. As a business owner and builder, I get to experience the entire creation process, from conceptual design to selecting and quantifying materials and assembling and installing them. Ensuring stability throughout construction is a journey to completion. The process of building a house makes me think about how He also builds us.

Let's take a look at Hebrews 3:4, which highlights that Jesus is even greater than Moses:

> *For Jesus has been counted worthy of more glory than Moses—as much more glory as the builder of a house has more honor than the house itself. (For every house is built by someone, but the builder of all things is God). —Hebrews 3:3-4 (ESV)*

At the time this was written, the Jews viewed Moses as one of the greatest and most powerful figures to ever live. He was a man through whom God displayed incredible miracles. Moses stepped forward into his calling, parting the Red Sea, bringing plagues upon Egypt, and even using his staff to draw water from a rock. These acts are crazy to think about and unlike anything we see today. Yet, even Moses, with all his greatness, was still a man in need of refinement.

When Moses disobeyed God by striking the rock with his rod to produce water instead of speaking to it as God had commanded, he acted out of frustration and took matters into his own hands. That moment of disobedience cost him the opportunity to enter the Promised Land and see the completion of the vision he had worked so hard for. It was a powerful reminder that even Moses, despite being chosen by God and doing extraordinary things, needed God to work on him, shape him, and hold him accountable.

And then Jesus came and introduced Himself as someone greater than Moses. While Moses brought the Law, Jesus brought grace and truth. Where Moses delivered his people out of physical bondage, Jesus came to free all people from spiritual bondage. It's a shift that reminds us not only of Jesus's greatness but also of our need to be continually shaped by Him. This tells me we must always approach life with the perspective that God is constantly working on us, shaping our character, refining our spirit, and guiding us step by step toward the ultimate finish line He's prepared for us. Even the greatest among us need God's hand to guide and grow them, and Jesus is that guiding presence for us all.

This book ultimately revolves around perspective and serving a higher purpose, acknowledging that there's a bigger picture at the beginning and end of everything. This has been the main focus in our journey of building a business.

As a builder, I am passionate about constructing things, so building a business was a natural fit. Whether it's building a house or a company, it aligns with how He created me and how I'm wired. I'm excited to share my journey throughout this book, the lessons I learned, and the insights gained along the way in this unique opportunity to be open and vulnerable.

I'm happy you made it this far. I want to emphasize the importance of **reading the last chapter right after this one** because it is crucial for understanding this topic of perspective. I hope you will recognize the importance of following the flow of His timing and the way He orchestrates things in every aspect of your life, whether it's starting a business, stepping out into your calling, or dealing with challenges and uncertainties. It emphasizes the need to position yourself before Him, acknowledging His ultimate authority as the Builder of All Things, and trusting in His plans for you. I hope you'll join me on the climb.

> **SONG PAIRING:** "Background" by Lecrae
> *Rehab* (Album)[5]

---

[5] Lecrae, vocalist, "Background," by Alex Medina, George Ramirez, et al., released September 28, 2010, track 13 on *Rehab*, Reach Records.

CHAPTER 2

THE SHIPMATE:
Two Boats

Two Are Better Than One

"We've worked hard all night and haven't caught anything."
—Luke 5:5

WASHING THE NETS

Back in 2014, during my third year as an owner in the construction business journey, I hit a roadblock where the fish weren't biting, financially speaking. The cash flow for our business wasn't sufficient to sustain new projects. Either I wasn't charging enough, or I didn't have the next level of license required to get the type of projects needed to sustain the ongoing costs that kept piling up. At that point, I realized it was time to step back and reevaluate the company as a whole.

By 2015, I decided to collaborate with my sister-in-law and brother-in-law, contemplating whether to weather the storm of our company or pivot into a new direction entirely. While I didn't close our business down completely, I recognized the need to rethink my approach. It was a difficult time for Tiffany and me. She was juggling three part-time jobs and raising our four kids while I was working long hours with my team, swinging hammers. I was struggling without the necessary administrative support, office space, and vehicles essential for running a construction business the way I wanted. It was becoming tough.

I found myself empathizing with the fishermen in Luke 5 who had been tirelessly fishing all night without much success. They said, "We've worked hard all night and haven't caught anything" (verse 4). I, too, had come to a point where I felt completely drained—physically, mentally, and financially. I didn't want to give up, but I realized I needed support. I lacked the resources, connections, and contractor licenses required to keep the company afloat. I was questioning if God really wanted us to have this company.

After three years of running the construction business, I felt like I was at the point of washing the nets and parking the boat. In fishing, "washing the nets" is what you do when you're done for the day. You've cast your lines, pulled up whatever you could, and now you're cleaning up. It's that moment when you're ready to call it quits and bring the boat in. In business, it's that same feeling. You've tried everything you know, pushed as hard as you can, and still, things just aren't working out. You're tired, and you're thinking, *Maybe it's time to quit.*

Although I didn't sail away from our business entirely, I found myself in a tough spot. I was pouring all my time and energy into work, logging long hours, losing touch with my kids, drifting apart from my wife, and even feeling disconnected from the church community. I felt more alone than ever before.

Have you ever felt like this? Where the busyness of everything begins to feel overwhelming, like drowning in an endless sea? Things don't seem to be falling into place, and the weight of it all makes you feel lost and desperate.

As a young, first-time business owner, I was hitting a wall. I mean, if the money is not there, bills and workers can't get paid. What else could I do? I thought I was doing everything right. I had stepped out in faith, trusting that God had assigned this wall to climb. I was honoring God and serving our clients with integrity and quality, but I felt like I must not have been running a well-oiled machine, and it might be time to wash the nets and hang up the ropes.

This season of bringing the boat (business) to shore was a time of seeking God for a new direction. I could deeply relate to the fishermen, sharing the same disappointments.

At the beginning of that fishing story, it says, "[Jesus] saw two boats by the lake, but the fishermen had gone out of them and were washing their nets" (Luke 5:2, ESV). What resonated with me about the story is how the fishermen, after a hard day's work and no success, had given up by the time they got back to shore. They were already cleaning their nets, mentally closing the chapter on that challenging day. Clocking out. Then this Man steps up and says, "Put out into deep water and let down the nets for a catch." Simon (who was also called Peter) answered, "Master, we've worked hard all night and haven't caught anything" (Luke 5:4, ESV).

From my years as a carpenter and then as a superintendent, I know this: at the end of a long, exhausting day, you don't look a worker in the eye and tell them to dig out the tools they just cleaned up, wrapped up, and stored for the night. It's about respect, right? You know they've given their all, and there's something unspoken that says, *You did good today. We're done, fellas.* That's how you build trust and show them their hard work matters. But the lead fisherman, Peter, answered, "But because you say so, I will let down the nets" (Luke 5:5, ESV).

There comes a point when we all feel like we want to give up, having exhausted every effort and resource of ours to accomplish the task at hand. These moments can feel so discouraging. I was experiencing this firsthand with our company.

Imagine a modern-day perspective: You're a small business owner pouring everything into your work. The late nights, the constant flow of projects, the endless to-do lists just won't let up. And despite all the effort, it feels like you're hitting a wall. Sales are sluggish, projects are slipping through your fingers, and every day, it seems harder to keep things on track. You're exhausted and at the point of "washing the nets" and clocking out. You've tried every approach you know, yet the results just aren't there.

Then, one evening, someone close to you, someone who's been watching you grind, offers an idea. There's something in their voice that catches you off guard like they can see beyond what you're struggling with right now. They suggest something that seems almost too simple to make a difference, like in Luke 5, where this Teacher (translated as "master" in some versions of the Bible) named Jesus tells the fishermen to cast their nets one more time, and this one small change brought a result they didn't expect, a catch beyond their wildest dreams: "When they had done so, they caught such a large number of fish that their nets began to break" (Luke 5:6, ESV).

Sometimes, a breakthrough comes from the person who knows you best, someone who sees your journey from a different angle and nudges you toward that next step. And in that moment, you realize this isn't just about the advice; it's about the quiet strength and insight of someone who's walking this path with you, ready to help you find your way when you're close to giving up.

Taking a year-long pause from our company in 2015 to work with my brother-in-law's company perfectly mirrored this story. When we face these junctures in business or even in our calling, there are two paths we can take. We can rely on our own strength, or we can let Jesus in our boat because from the time Jesus saw the fishermen and when they brought in the haul of fish, something else had happened: "[Jesus] got into one of the boats, the one belonging to [Peter], and asked him to put out a little from shore" (Luke 5:3, ESV).

The story of Peter meeting Jesus really started to unfold and speak to me. I felt as though God was speaking directly to me in Luke 5:3 when Jesus asked him to put out the boat a little from shore.

> **TO TRULY INVITE JESUS ON BOARD, WE'VE GOT TO CLEAR OUT THE CLUTTER.**

Reflecting on my journey, I've come to believe God led me to a place where I had to empty myself. In business, it's easy to get wrapped up in managing everything alone. We push hard, thinking it's all on us, and we forget to lean on God, the real Owner. It's like we're so focused on keeping it all together that we lose sight of who's truly in charge. But God knows when to step in, just like Jesus knew the perfect time to show up for Peter.

Picture Peter that day, standing at the water's edge, his boat pulled up, nets washed, and everything packed away after a long, fruitless night. He'd already called it quits, loaded his tools, and was ready to go home. Then, here comes Jesus, asking him to take the boat back out. Imagine the scene—he had to reload everything, pull back out, and make space for Jesus. But in doing so, he gave Jesus a platform to teach and reach others.

For us, it's the same. To truly invite Jesus on board, we've got to clear out the clutter. Sometimes, it's not just about clearing space physically but letting go of control, releasing our worries, and setting aside our pride. God might even allow seasons that force us to let go, stripping away distractions so we can see Him more clearly. That's what He was doing with me—guiding me to a point where I had to say, "I can't do this on my own."

Just like Peter, we sometimes need to be brought to shore, to a place where we're willing to empty ourselves. Only then, when we've made room, can God truly step in and take us to deeper waters. It's in those moments, with an open heart and an empty boat, that He fills us with faith and purpose beyond what we ever could have imagined.

TWO BOATS

Building a business can feel like a constant uphill battle. No matter how much you plan, there are days when it feels like everything's working against you, and you're ready to throw in the towel. I've been there, when cash flow is tight, progress feels stalled, and it seems like no matter what you try, the nets keep coming up empty. There's no magic fix for those days, but I believe God gave me something better than a quick fix. He showed me the power of a second boat.

In Luke 5, there were two boats on the shore, not just one. God started speaking to me through that image, showing me that to truly set out again—to rebuild, relaunch, or go deeper—I couldn't do it alone. Just like those two boats worked together to bring in the catch, we need the right people alongside us to fill the gaps we can't cover alone. We need people who can stand in where we're weak, who can offer fresh perspectives, accountability, or just an extra set of hands to keep us going when we're ready to clock out.

When I served in the Navy, I learned about a bond that's like no other. We called each other shipmates. A shipmate isn't just someone on the same boat; they're family out on the water. They're the person you can count on, the one you trust, the one who's got your back no matter what comes your way. They're right there with you, shoulder to shoulder, putting in the work when the seas are rough and celebrating with you when everything's running smooth.

A shipmate isn't just along for the ride; they're all in, taking on their part so you can handle yours. They know the stakes, they know the mission, and they're fully committed to it. In the end, a shipmate is more than a coworker or just another body on board. They're part of the heartbeat of the team. They're right there, fully invested in the journey with you.

For me, it was time for me to find my shipmate. Someone who could walk with me, not only in business but in life. Someone who could lift me up spiritually and practically. We all need a second boat, whether it's a business partner, a mentor, a teammate, or even a friend who's in it with you, boots on the ground, facing the same challenges. God knows that none of us were built to do this alone.

When we look at some of the biggest, most successful companies and partnerships in history, we see the power of a shipmate. Walt Disney had Ub Iwerks. Disney was the dreamer, the visionary who saw worlds in his mind, but it was Iwerks who sketched the very first lines of Mickey Mouse. Iwerks was the artist, character designer, and inventor who turned Disney's ideas into something real. Without him, Disney's vision might have stayed just that, a vision.

Look at Steve Jobs and Steve Wozniak. Jobs was the face and the visionary force behind Apple, but Wozniak was the one who made that vision possible. He was the engineer, the one who built the first Apple computer, putting Jobs's ideas into a product that changed the world. Jobs needed Woz to ground his vision in reality, to make it something people could hold in their hands.

Even in sports, where we often celebrate the star player, we know no one wins alone. Michael Jordan is a legend, but he didn't win six championships on his own. He had Scottie Pippen, someone just as fierce, who could fill in the gaps, handle the pressure, and play the game in a way that allowed Jordan to shine. They needed each other to reach the heights they did.

These examples show us that the greatest accomplishments rarely happen solo. Behind every visionary is a shipmate in some shape or form who complements them, who fills the spaces they can't fill alone. In business, sports, or life, we need those "second boats," those teammates who bring strengths where we lack, who help turn dreams into something real, and who stand beside us when the waters get rough.

Solomon, known as one of the wisest guys to ever walk the earth, understood the power of having a second boat and the value of having a true shipmate. He was a king in ancient Israel, famous for his wisdom, wealth, and the deep insights he shared about life. When he wrote about the strength of two people working together, he knew what he was talking about.

He understood that life's battles are easier with someone by your side, someone to lift you up when things get tough.

> *"Two are better than one, because they have a good return for their labor: If either of them falls down, one can help the other up."*
> —Ecclesiastes 4:9-10

I'm not saying you can't do it alone, but at least in my position and where God wanted to take us, I needed the help. I needed the second boat. Some of the greatest companies in history could navigate and grow when they formed partnerships, developed councils, and had accountability with teams. We all have different gifts, and when you can bridge those gifts together, you're just so much stronger.

Tiffany and I love watching movies together. I usually ask her what genre she is in the mood for, and she shares and lets me choose the movie or show. Over all the years of watching movies with her, sci-fi wins for the top requested genre. Her Uncle Glen used to watch her and her siblings growing up and always watched a ton of sci-fi movies together. One was *The Planet of the Apes*.[6] Tiffany and I have watched the recent trilogy together a few times. To this day, she thinks it's comical that the apes ride horses.

If you haven't seen the movie *Rise of the Planet of the Apes*, it's about a young chimpanzee named Caesar, who has been genetically modified to enhance his intelligence. Over time,

---

6 Tim Burton, *Planet of the Apes* trilogy (2001; Los Angeles, CA: 20th Century Studios).

Caesar begins to realize his own intelligence and capabilities, far surpassing those of a typical ape.

As Caesar grows, he witnesses the mistreatment of apes in captivity and starts to feel a sense of injustice. Caesar experiences human cruelty firsthand. In this challenging environment, he speaks in sign language to an orangutan named Maurice. Caesar holds one stick with two hands, breaks it, and says, "Ape alone weak." He then grabs several sticks with two hands and shows that the sticks can't break and says, "Ape together strong."[7] This phrase became a silly mantra for us, knowing together we are stronger.

While working with my brother-in-law's company, I poured myself into it, handling the administrative side, managing projects, throwing all my energy into helping them grow, treating it like it was my own. But honestly, I was wearing myself out. I was pushing so hard, overextending myself, and Tiffany saw it. She could see the burnout creeping in, and she knew I needed something to make this all sustainable.

Tiffany started researching ways to help, looking for some kind of organizational tool for builders that might make things easier. She found a CRM program and thought it could be the answer. But in my "I've got this" mindset, I thanked her, told her I had it under control, and brushed it off. She insisted, though, and because she's my wife, I figured, alright, I'll at least give it a chance. So, I did.

---

7   Rupert Wyatt, *Rise of the Planet of the Apes* (August 5, 2011; Los Angeles, CA: 20th Century Studios).

> **SOMETIMES, THE BREAKTHROUGH YOU'RE LOOKING FOR COMES WHEN YOU'RE HUMBLE ENOUGH TO LISTEN TO THE PEOPLE AROUND YOU.**

The more I looked into that program, the more I realized it was like that moment when Jesus told Peter to throw the net out one more time. Suddenly, it was like God downloaded a vision straight into me, filling me with ideas. This program was the tool we'd been missing, the answer to why we were hitting roadblocks and why we hadn't been performing the way we could have.

Now, I'm not saying this program is a one-size-fits-all solution. What I am saying is that sometimes, the breakthrough you're looking for comes when you're humble enough to listen to the people around you—Tiffany's insight, her belief in the potential she saw, aligned with the culture and vision we needed to keep moving forward. Being open to her help was the game-changer.

I realized I needed Tiffany like I needed air. There I was, pushing myself to the edge, trying to juggle a million things on my own, convinced I had to handle it all. But deep down, I knew something was off. I was burning out, stretched so thin that I couldn't see straight. When I realized that Tiffany was the one who needed to be by my side, I didn't hesitate. I asked her to leave her job at the airport, come on full-time, and help me relaunch our company. I even offered her a sign-on bonus to show how serious I was. Tiffany had a good thing going at Alaska Airlines in Honolulu—she had her routines, great benefits, and the freedom to hop on a plane to Japan or California whenever she wanted. But I laid it out for her, shared the struggles we were facing, and painted the vision of what we could build together.

When she took that leap and joined me, she brought more than just her time—she brought skills and a fresh perspective that changed everything. She built us an online portal to streamline operations, reorganized our finances, kickstarted our admin processes, and came up with creative solutions that pushed us forward. She was the VP I needed, pulling together the necessary resources and ideas from every direction. Tiffany wasn't just there to fill a spot; she was there to help me steer this ship, and she made us stronger in ways I couldn't have done alone.

I had to sit down with my brother-in-law, Randy, and my sister-in-law, Kristy, and share the news that Tiffany and I were ready to relaunch our company again on our own. I thanked them for partnering with us and for believing in us during that season. They may not have fully understood our decision at the time, but looking back now, they see where we were headed. They have even expressed how proud they are of us for trusting God's lead and stepping out in faith.

So, we began again. Our first office was nothing fancy. We set up in my son's old room on the second floor. Tiffany took charge of office operations, hired our oldest daughter, Kiko, and gave me some breathing room to focus on other tasks. We divided up responsibilities. Tiffany handled one side of the business while I went full force in getting our contractor's license in Hawai'i and growing the other parts.

When we officially launched in 2016 and got licensed, we could feel God's blessing over everything we were building. It was as if everything was aligning perfectly, and His hand was guiding us every step of the way.

That was just the beginning. Partnering with Tiffany was the first big step in building something bigger than either of us could have done alone. It set us up to scale, to build teams, and to lay down a legacy. One step, one shipmate, and one leap of faith at a time.

> **WHAT JESUS WAS TELLING ME WAS TO GO BACK OUT BUT WITH A SHIPMATE.**

Tiffany brought excellence and experience to the company. You see, she is a huge Disney park fan. She went as an adult for the first time and fell in love with the experience and excellence of everything in the park. She recognized that from the moment you step into the park, you can tell everything was designed with intention. The themes pull you in, the smells and music are perfectly crafted, and the cast of characters and performers are always in the right place at the right time. Every detail, from the food to the rides, was built with a level of quality and care that's hard to miss. The whole place feels like it was made to immerse you in something unforgettable, like every corner was designed to bring the magic to life. She had the same desire as I do to use that type of experience in our business. We both agreed and felt inspired to deliver God's excellence to the highest degree possible.

Looking back at the scripture, when Peter followed the lead of Jesus out of obedience and threw the net, they were truly blessed. What Jesus was telling me was to go back out but with a shipmate.

I'm not saying all spouses are destined to be business partners, but I am saying two is better than one. Once we set sail again, we experienced what those fishermen did when they let Jesus on their boat, allowed Him to use their boat as a platform, and signaled the second boat for help: "So they signaled their *partners* in the other boat to come and *help* them, and they came and filled *both* boats so full that they began to sink" (Luke 5:7, ESV, emphasis added).

Looking back now, I'm beyond thankful that I had the humility to listen to Tiffany's advice and to follow God's lead in partnering with her. She was the piece I didn't even know I was missing. Because I trusted her, and because I trusted God's nudge, everything started to come together in ways I couldn't have made happen on my own.

From a business standpoint, the blessings from obedience were just as Peter felt when his boat and the second boat were so full that they began to sink. Since Tiffany came on board, we've been able to create a culture and performance-driven environment that has taken us and our team to new levels we never imagined possible.

> **SONG PAIRING:** "All I Need Is You" by Lecrae
> *Anomaly* (Album)[8]

---

8   Lecrae, vocalist, "All I Need Is You," by Dustin Adrian Bowie, Joseph Ryan Prielozny, et al., September 9, 2014, track 11 on *Anomaly*, Reach Records.

PART 2

BEGINNING THE COURSE

CHAPTER 3

THE STREAM:
Heart of a King

*The Destination Is
Already Determined*

*"The king's heart is a stream of water in the hand
of the LORD; he turns it wherever he will."*
—Proverbs 21:1 (ESV)

NAVIGATING DEEP WATERS

When Tiffany and I partnered up, it was like setting sail with the wind at our backs. Those early years were fun and full of great energy. Before we knew it, we were running full throttle. Projects kept rolling in, clients were happy, and our Yelp page was flooded with five-star reviews. Each one felt like a confirmation that we were on the right track, and it wasn't long before we were the "go-to" construction company on the island. The phone wouldn't stop ringing, and each call was another step toward building something we were proud of.

> **THE WORK WAS POURING IN, BUT I WAS LOSING SIGHT OF WHERE WE WERE ACTUALLY HEADED.**

Our team and culture were growing too, and it felt like we were creating something real. We had people who shared our commitment and who worked with the same grind and heart we did. Our crew was close like family, and the culture was growing and strengthening around everything we stood for.

But as the business picked up speed, I realized I was out in the middle of this vast ocean of opportunity, with no clear map to guide our next steps. It started to feel like landing more jobs was all we were chasing, but that wasn't our true purpose. We had momentum, but I had no real direction for how to manage the growth or sustain it. The work was pouring in, but I was losing sight of where we were actually headed. I was passionate about what we were building and loved being able to provide for our team but just stacking up projects wasn't hitting the deeper purpose I felt in my heart. We were busy, sure, but we weren't steering in a clear direction. And out there, in the vast ocean of business, that lack of focus on a purpose can weigh you and your team down fast.

Starting on this journey to build our business, there were days it felt like we were out in the middle of the ocean, deep waters all around us like we were lost at sea. The harder I tried to find our direction, the more lost I felt. I started paying attention, watching other businesses push hard to be the biggest and the best, always chasing that next level. So, I would jump in and sign up for business coaching sessions to learn more, take courses, and listen to all these entrepreneurs sharing their success stories online. I tried everything, from their step-by-step diagrams to their motivation techniques. But after a while, I realized a lot of it was just surface-level stuff, temporary boosts that didn't really go deep.

I got swept up in this constant push to grow—more projects, more jobs for our employees, and more revenue—always adding to the load but never feeling like I truly knew what I was aiming for.

Imagine being out in the middle of the ocean on a boat with no digital tech, no GPS, no tools to guide you. Just you, the endless water, and the sky. No clear direction, no way to tell where you're headed—just drifting, completely at the mercy of the waves. Out in the open ocean, there's nothing familiar to ground you, no landmarks, no signs to reassure you. It's just miles and miles of blue, stretching out in every direction. The challenge isn't just physical; it's also mental. Out there, it's you and the hope that you're still on course. There's no safety net, no sight of land to steady you. The vastness of it all can start messing with your head, making you question if you're even going the right way.

I did two tours out at sea in the Navy, so I know what it's like to be surrounded by nothing but miles and miles of water. I was on a 567-foot missile cruiser, close to 10,000 tons, cutting through the Pacific Ocean at over thirty knots. Imagine a ship that massive, pushing through the ocean for nearly a month straight, with nothing but horizon in every direction. After a while, you almost feel like you're becoming part of the sea itself. The constant hum of the engines, the endless water, and the isolation make you question where you are in the world. Each second feels like it pulls you further from any sense of grounding, like you're slipping away from the familiar world. Out there, you've got no clue where you are unless the captain fills you in. You're just trusting, hoping you're headed the right way, and relying on him to keep you on course.

As we sailed from Hawai'i toward the Persian Gulf, we passed over some of the deepest parts of the ocean. There's a spot just south of Guam called the Challenger Deep, nearly seven miles down to the ocean floor. You look over the ship's edge, trying to wrap your head around what's beneath you, but it's like staring into infinity. The water is so deep that it feels like the ocean has no bottom, like you're just hanging there between the surface and a dark, endless void.

Hovering over depths we still haven't fully explored makes you realize how small and temporary you are in the face of something so vast. It's humbling to know we haven't even conquered those depths yet. The further out you go, the deeper it gets, and the more you realize—this ocean, like life itself—has layers that go way beyond what you can see or fully understand.

Just as navigating the vastness of the ocean can leave you feeling lost and overwhelmed, so, too, can the journey of building a business, both filled with depths that challenge your sense of direction and understanding.

Being over the Challenger Deep didn't just make me feel lost; it hit me with this raw fear, this sense that I couldn't even trust what was under us. It's one thing to be out in open water with no land in sight, but floating over a place where the ocean floor is seven miles down? That's a whole different level. You start thinking about what's below, the unknowns lurking in that darkness. It's like looking into an endless abyss, and suddenly, even the water beneath you feels unstable. That deep, empty space beneath makes you question everything you thought was solid, and it brings up this feeling that you're completely ungrounded, as if you're hanging over a world you don't understand.

In a way, that same sense of deep uncertainty started hitting me in my own life. Balancing the weight of my responsibilities felt overwhelming, as if I was being torn between two worlds that both meant so much to me—my personal life and business—but I just couldn't give my all to either one. Being unavailable for my family at home left me feeling stretched thin and disconnected. The weight of financial pressure was starting to suffocate me. It was overwhelming, and I knew I couldn't handle it on my own. I had to let go, step back from the helm, and find something greater than me to guide us through.

Every business coach I signed up with looked at our data, checked out our operations, and was like, "You guys are killing it." They'd say, "Honestly, I'm trying to find ways to help, but your systems, your SOPs, the way you're running things—it's at a level of excellence we don't usually see."

We were checking all the boxes, but I kept wondering, do other business owners hit a crossroads like this too? Is it really all just about success, pushing revenue, growing profits, and letting the business take over your life? Where's the balance between success and purpose, family and significance? My heart wasn't in the lane of just making money and being known. I wasn't built to just build for the sake of building. I needed something deeper. After years of having behind-the-door conversations with other business owners, I feel there are many more people out there who can relate.

I reached a point where I felt completely overwhelmed, like I was drowning in the deep waters of the business world. The more I watched other entrepreneurs define success, the more I realized their version didn't align with what I felt in my heart. Scrolling through endless "secrets to success" reels on Instagram only left me feeling even more disconnected and turned off by the whole business success scene.

I didn't want to pursue that kind of success. I wanted something real, something that felt genuine and in line with my values. That version of success that's constantly pushed online—money, status, all of that—just wasn't what I was after. I wanted to build something that truly mattered to us, something that reflected what we actually believed. We are in this American culture that often says money and status are the keys to influence and power, but I believe that God is the key provider of our resources and that He positions us for significant impact. That's when I started digging deeper, looking for true purpose. And that's where this journey took a whole new turn.

KINGS OF YESTERDAY, ENTREPRENEURS OF TODAY

The year 2018 was a major turning point in my life. I started feeling this deep motivation to dive into the lives of historical figures from the Bible, people who, in their time, were leaders, decision-makers, and even business-like figures. I spent hours studying these stories, and each time, I was struck by how closely they connected to real business principles. It wasn't just spiritual insight. It was like opening a guidebook for leadership, vision, and growth.

The more I dug in, the more I started seeing these ancient principles as tools for finding my true purpose, showing me who I was meant to be, not just in life but in the work I do. It was eye-opening, bringing a sense of clarity to my journey that I'd never felt before.

There was one verse that really sparked something within me, a line that shifted everything. It came from the book of Isaiah, and it hit me deeply:

> *"Are not my commanders all kings?"*
> —Isaiah 10:8 (ESV)

This question brought a whole new perspective to me, especially because, in Hawaiian culture, a king isn't just a figurehead. A king is a ruler, a decision-maker, someone who oversees both the land and business affairs of the people. Seeing this idea of kingship through that lens helped me connect some dots between God's view of leadership and what it means to be an entrepreneur. I started noticing how ancient kings actually had similar roles and faced the same kinds of challenges as today's entrepreneurs. Like today's entrepreneurs, they needed to think big, manage high-level decisions, and balance the risks and rewards of leadership. This realization inspired me to study these biblical kings even more closely, especially how God guided them.

As I read through books like Chronicles, Kings, and Samuel, I saw how God held ultimate control. He guided kings, sometimes steering them towards greatness, other times letting them face ruin when they ignored His guidance. The insights I was uncovering felt like discovering a treasure chest full of wisdom. I started imagining that if I swapped out the word "king" with "entrepreneur" or "business owner," the lessons still fit perfectly today. It was an incredible moment, like finding a treasure map for leading a business with meaning and purpose.

> **IT'S LIKE THE BUILDER OF ALL THINGS GAVE ME AN UNDERSTANDING OF THE KEY TO HIS HEART.**

As I continued to study the kings in the Scriptures, I was super intrigued by the life of Solomon, known as one of the wealthiest and most successful kings in history. While monetary wealth wasn't the primary goal or measure of success for me in business, nobody could overlook Solomon's great wealth, wisdom, and the accolades he received.

While I was studying Solomon, God opened my eyes to something that just clicked. Solomon, for those who aren't familiar, wrote much of Proverbs, a book in the Bible full of powerful, straightforward sayings packed with wisdom about life, work, leadership, and faith. Proverbs is Solomon's legacy, where he shares everything he learned.

As I was reading, one of these proverbs stood out. It was like God was connecting the dots for me. The revelation of this scripture changed everything about how I looked at my business journey. It gave me a new vision to reflect upon. It gave me a new perception of how I see the journey. It gave me the tools I needed to realign how we did things. It redefined what success meant for me. It changed my whole perspective on business and life completely. It served as my new compass, guiding me toward a fresh perspective on success. It was like new GPS coordinates had been entered, steering me in the right direction and clearing my mind of the overwhelming amount of worldly knowledge I had accumulated through my earlier days of research. It's like the Builder of All Things gave me an understanding of the key to His heart. It's the key that unlocked the door to this entire book.

FROM THE OCEAN TO THE STREAM

> *"The king's heart is like a stream of water directed by the LORD; he guides it wherever he pleases."*
> —Proverbs 21:1 (NLT)

What caught my attention in this scripture were the words "king's heart." This is what my heart had been seeking the whole time, and I didn't even know it. I'd ask myself, *How should I position my heart through all of this?* Especially a king's heart or, let's say, the heart of an entrepreneur or leader. I was navigating the ocean with my eyes and my mind, but my heart wasn't connecting. I was following knowledge and what I could see, but deep down, what I really wanted was to find meaning, something that made a real impact. I needed to understand how to align my heart with that purpose, to let it guide me instead of just going through the motions of what I believed to be successful.

"The king's heart is like a stream of water." Hmm, *stream*? That word struck me right away because it's so different from an ocean. A stream is nothing like an ocean, actually. Growing up in Peoria, Illinois, known as the River City, I was always around the Illinois River. We all knew exactly where that river started and where it ended. Now, after years spent out on the ocean in the Navy and living here in Hawai'i, I've learned firsthand how different these two bodies of water really are.

Then, like a lightbulb moment, it hit me! Unlike the vast, endless ocean where you can't see the end, a stream has a clear path and a set destination. I realized that in the world of entrepreneurship, so many people are out there like explorers in the middle of the ocean, searching for success, wealth, or fame. But a stream? A stream already has a path carved out by God, with a destination in mind.

Then came another revelation. It was like taking a peek at the end of the Golden State Warriors basketball game shared in chapter 10—the victory is already there; we've already won. Suddenly, I could now see that I didn't have to worry about the unknowns at the end of my business pursuits. My whole view of success shifted. Now, I could rest, trusting that I was on a path with a purpose and that God had already marked the destination.

With God as my partner in ownership and me as the steward of the business, I now know that His hand is on the business, holding it steady in the stream. I can finally rest, knowing He's the one who establishes the vision, sets the current in the stream, and leads us forward. He's paving the way, so I don't have to rely on my own strength, drifting around like I'm lost at sea. Instead, I can lean on Him for direction and strength, trusting that He's guiding every step.

"Therefore, do not worry about tomorrow, for tomorrow will worry about itself. Each day has enough trouble of its own."
—Matthew 6:34

The revelation I received brought me peace. I feel like I am in a sturdy boat floating down a tranquil stream as I visualize myself in the palm of God's hand, trusting that the stream will guide me. My GPS is locked in. All I need to do is focus on the present moment, navigate around the small rocks that may appear in front of me, appreciate the beauty of the surrounding scenery, and find joy in God's presence right there with me. Now, it's all about embracing the journey rather than fixating solely on the destination.

A sense of relief settled within me, shifting my perspective from the ocean to the stream. Success isn't about piling up achievements or commas in profits. It's about finding real meaning in the journey itself, letting each step be part of something greater. Knowing there's victory waiting lets me enjoy the ride and trust that every moment has a purpose that goes way beyond what the world might call "success." Instead of seeing success as just hitting a target, it's about making an impact and fulfilling a purpose. It's about cherishing the process, the connections we make, the experiences we share, and the skills we inherit. The outcome is His, not mine, and that brings us peace.

Even looking back, I recognize my whole life is like a stream. He's been guiding me the whole way. Now that I'm aware of it, I can see where those doors opened and closed along the way, and I am thankful for each one. Some construction projects seemed right to pursue and made the most sense, but the doors closed. We are truly grateful that our eyes have been opened to how God operates and how He has been guiding us along His stream the whole time.

The application for us became easy. As we pursued new projects and clients, we made it a point to pray for God to open the doors He wanted to open and close the ones He wanted to close, keeping us aligned with His stream. We trusted Him every step of the way and found joy in the outcomes.

Sometimes, along the way, God graciously reveals fragments of the destination ahead to offer us hope, encouragement, and clarity. It's like slowly uncovering a grand puzzle, with each piece bringing us closer to seeing the full picture. Then, one day, we reach that final destination, and the realization dawns upon us: the mission is accomplished. Then we take off again, ready to embrace the next chapter that awaits us.

This perspective can be applied to every aspect of life—whether it's how you view your marriage, your business, or even your role as a leader. The term "king" could easily be interchanged with "husband," "business owner," "coach," or any position of authority. It might seem like a simple concept, not overly profound, but for me, it's been a life-changing revelation. It has truly opened my eyes to understand that anything I consider a success comes from appreciating and finding beauty in every moment, with God's hand as the foundation, no matter the circumstance.

Easier said than done, which we will see in the upcoming chapters, as the world and the enemy will do everything to distract you from such a simple task.

> *"And we know that in all things God works for the good of those who love him, who have been called according to his purpose."*
> —Romans 8:28

Every experience, whether it's a challenge or a win, is connected to the bigger picture of our lives, like a stream guiding us forward. Imagine it like this: you're navigating a boat down a stream, and a rock bumps you to the left. At first, it's just an obstacle. But maybe that little nudge actually steers you clear of a low-hanging branch up ahead on the right, one you wouldn't have seen coming. That bump wasn't just a random inconvenience—it was part of keeping you on track.

> **SEEING GOD AS THE TRUE OWNER OF YOUR COMPANY LIFTS THAT HEAVY WEIGHT OFF YOUR SHOULDERS.**

In real life, it's the same thing. Let's say a big project at work falls through, or you lose a client you thought was a sure thing. At the moment, it feels like a setback, maybe even a failure. But then, because of that shift, a better opportunity comes along—a client who's a better fit or a project that's more in line with what you want to do. That loss, that "bump," actually helped guide you toward something that fits the bigger plan. Every little twist and turn has a purpose, even if we can't see it right away.

So, when we finally reach the destination we've been working toward, it's not just about the end result. It's about understanding and appreciating all those moments that nudged us along the way. They were all part of a larger plan that got us to exactly where we were meant to be.

Here's the truth, CEO to CEO: when you let God reposition your heart, you'll experience success on a different level. Not the kind the world chases with endless goals and milestones, but something real, something rooted in purpose. You'll no longer be driven by pressure or status. Instead, you'll build something that truly matters, knowing the One who called you to lead has already set the destination.

It's about letting go of control. Seeing God as the true owner of your company lifts that heavy weight off your shoulders. You're still responsible for stewardship and leadership, but you don't have to carry it alone. That shift—seeing yourself as a steward, not just an owner—frees you up to lead with purpose, not just profit. It changes how you handle every decision and every challenge.

Your drive shifts from ambition to calling. Instead of proving something to the world, you're fulfilling something greater, and with that comes a new kind of contentment. Every success, every challenge, every lesson—it's all part of how God's equipping you and drawing you closer to His vision for your leadership.

So, here's the key: don't just focus on getting somewhere. Embrace every step as part of where He's taking you. Trust that every part of the journey—even the obstacles and redirections—is part of His growth plan. These redirections aren't setbacks; they're opportunities for new doors to open, for you to see possibilities you may have missed otherwise.

When you align your heart with His and lead with trust, your business is no longer just work. It becomes a calling. God moves you from profit to purpose and from ambition to impact. And here's the best part: you're free to enjoy the journey with confidence, knowing He's already secured the destination.

Lead with that kind of heart, and you'll find you're not just building a business. You're building a legacy, guided by purpose, and centered on the God who set this course for you long before you took the first step.

> **SONG PAIRING:** "Journey" by Lecrae
> CC4 (Album)[9]

---

9   Lecrae, vocalist, "Journey," by Donald Cannon, Harold Allen, et al., February 24, 2022, track 12 on *CC4*, Reach Records.

CHAPTER 4

THE SAIL:
The Wind Blows

Stepping Into Your Calling

"The wind blows wherever it pleases. You hear its sound, but you cannot tell where it comes from or where it is going. So it is with everyone born of the Spirit."
—John 3:8

LISTENING TO LIFE'S WHISPERS

In life, there comes a moment when we each feel called to step into our purpose toward something greater. I think deep down, we all hope for the day we finally reach the door that leads to our purpose and enter. We're all wired to long for this purpose and for meaning in our lives. Eventually, whether it's through struggles, victories, or moments of clarity, we'll find ourselves standing before this metaphorical door inscribed with the words, "You are called for this." It's the moment everything clicks, and we realize we were made for something bigger all along.

How do you find it? How do you know when it's time to step through? That door doesn't just appear out of nowhere. It's carved into your story by the moments that shape you. It's in the quiet tug on your heart when something feels right, like it was made just for you. It's in the way your gifts seem to line up perfectly, like pieces of a puzzle finally coming together. It's in the hard lessons you've learned through struggle, the ones that made you stronger, wiser, and more certain of who you are. And it's in the pull you can't ignore, the one that draws you toward something bigger, something that matters.

You might not recognize it at first, but every step, every stumble, and every victory is leading you closer. And when you find yourself standing before that door, you'll feel it deep in your soul. It's not a coincidence. It's purpose calling your name.

Steve Jobs, one of my favorite entrepreneurs of my time, was a true game-changer who co-founded Apple and revolutionized the tech world. He didn't just create products like the iPhone, iPad, and Mac. He built a movement, blending creativity with functionality and making technology accessible to everyone. His vision pushed boundaries and inspired the world to "think differently." But even visionaries face setbacks. It's crazy to think about how he was removed from the very company he built. What seemed like a devastating blow became a turning point in his story. During this period, he founded a new company, NeXT, and was part of transforming Pixar, setting the stage for his incredible return to Apple.

I can imagine Steve Jobs's removal from Apple in 1985 was a deeply emotional and transformative experience for him. At just thirty years old, he had built the company from the ground up, only to find himself ousted from the organization he'd built and loved.

> **THERE WILL COME MOMENTS IN LIFE WHEN WE HAVE TO MAKE A CHOICE TO STEP THROUGH THE DOOR WITH FAITH OR STAY WHERE IT FEELS SAFE.**

In his 2005 Stanford commencement speech, Jobs referred to this period as a very public failure and admitted that he was devastated. He described feeling like he had let the previous generation of entrepreneurs down. Through this experience of being let go, Jobs rediscovered his passion for product design and technology, as well as his ambition to create meaningful, life-changing products. I truly believe that one day, he found himself standing before a metaphorical door of purpose with a sign that said, "You were destined for this; don't give up." When he looked back at that time, he said:

> *Getting fired from Apple was the best thing that could have ever happened to me. The heaviness of being successful was replaced by the lightness of being a*

beginner again.... It freed me to enter one of the most creative periods of my life.[10]

The emotional depth of being rejected by his own company made Steve Jobs reflect on his life and helped him discover who he was and what he was molded and created for. Jobs knew his life and purpose were tied to Apple because it was the intersection of his personal passion for innovation, his desire to finish what he had started, and his belief that he could lead the company to change the world in ways that no one else could. His return marked the beginning of Apple's transformation into one of the most valuable and influential companies in the world. Steve Jobs knew how to tap into his heart and intuition as he also revealed in the speech, "Have the *courage* to follow your heart and intuition. They somehow already know what you truly want to become."

Many people find it challenging to trust their gut feelings, but it's crucial to pay attention to them. These instincts are like your inner compass. Your subconscious pulls from everything you've been through—the wins, the losses, and the lessons you didn't even know you'd learned. It's that gut feeling, that split-second reaction when there's no time to overthink. It's not magic; it's your life speaking back to you, guiding your next step. The heart Steve Jobs is talking about here goes deeper than the physical organ or even identifying what you love. I believe it's what God has planted in you from birth, the experiences He has allowed into your life to align your intuition with your heart.

---

10 Steve Jobs, "2005 Stanford Commencement Address" (commencement speech, Stanford University, Stanford, CA, June 12, 2005).

Steve Jobs had an unshakable belief that he was destined for his role, like he was made for it. It was then that he stepped through this metaphorical door and returned to Apple in 1997.

Your work is going to fill a large part of your life, and the only way to be truly satisfied is to do what you believe is great work. And the only way to do great work is to love what you do. If you haven't found it yet, keep looking. Don't settle. As with all matters of the heart, you'll know when you find it.[11]

There will come moments in life when we have to make a choice to step through the door with faith or stay where it feels safe. But we can't settle, not until we walk through. When we do, when we embrace what we're meant for—what I call "our calling"—everything changes. Eventually, we turn around and see the back of that door. I believe the message will read and hit differently, saying: "You were chosen for this."

That word "chosen" is powerful. It's the moment when you look back on life, through all the twists and turns, and realize it was all meant to be. For me, it was every challenge I faced as a kid, the doors that slammed shut in college, the battles I fought in the military, all of it led me here. I remember the exact day I looked into my newborn baby's eyes and felt it in my soul. Not one moment of my life could have been different. Every step, every struggle, every victory brought me to that jewel in my hands. It's in those moments you know, without a doubt, you were chosen for this.

Your calling and purpose work in much the same way. There is a builder, the Builder of all Things, carefully shaping

---
11 Jobs, "2005 Stanford Commencement Address."

your path. Every step, every challenge, every moment is part of His work, leading you to those crossroads and intersections in life. Those moments when the door stands right in front of you, waiting for you to step through. It is your chance to trust the process and walk into what you were made for. But here is the key. You have to pay attention. Life whispers in subtle ways, guiding and shaping you through every experience, like the wind nudging a boat along the stream. Steering you toward the path you were always meant to take.

> *"I will instruct you and teach you in the way you should go; I will counsel you with my loving eye on you."*
> —Psalms 32:8

Our lives, like Steve Jobs's journey, are shaped by the experiences and challenges we face along the way, often taking unexpected turns that mold us into who we are meant to be. Just as Jobs faced setbacks and periods of reflection that ultimately led him back to Apple with a renewed sense of purpose, our own struggles and detours are part of the master plan, steering us toward the purpose we were always meant to fulfill. When he returned to Apple, he didn't just rebuild a company; he reimagined the future, creating products that turned dreams into reality and changed how we live, work, and dream.

THE BASKET IN THE STREAM

Just like Steve Jobs's life shows us how challenges can shape us for something greater, there's another story in the Bible about a man named Moses whose life started in chaos. Born at a time when his people were enslaved and their baby boys were being killed, Moses's life was in danger from the start. To save him, his mother placed him in a basket and set him afloat on a river, hoping for a miracle. Imagine that—a baby drifting down the water, completely vulnerable, yet carried by something bigger than chance. That moment marked the beginning of a journey that would change history, showing how even in uncertainty, we're being guided toward a greater purpose.

The incredible story starts with Moses's mother, Jochebed. She lived in a time when her people, the Israelites, were oppressed and Pharaoh, the king of Egypt, had ordered that all Hebrew baby boys be killed. Can you imagine the fear she must have felt when she gave birth to her son Moses? But instead of giving up, she made a bold choice. She crafted a basket and placed her baby inside. Then, with nothing but faith, she set that basket afloat on the Nile River, trusting that somehow her child would be protected.

Moses's sister, Miriam, watched over the basket as it drifted downstream. If you don't already know the story, here's where it takes an unexpected turn. Pharaoh's daughter, of all people, found the basket while she was bathing by the river. She heard the baby crying and felt compassion for him, even though she knew he was a Hebrew child. Instead of turning him away, she decided to adopt him and raise him as her own, giving him a life of privilege as an Egyptian prince.

It's wild to think about how this one moment of courage from Moses's mother set him on a path to becoming one of the most significant leaders in history. Raised in the very palace of the man who wanted him dead, Moses would one day rise to lead the Israelites to freedom. It all started with a mother's faith and a simple basket floating on the stream of a river.

Moses's mom had a purpose, and she owned it. She was called to give birth, protect her son during a time when baby boys were being hunted, and do whatever it took to save him. She didn't just sit back and hope; she got creative. She built a basket out of reeds, almost like a little boat, waterproofed it with tar, and placed her baby inside. But she didn't just toss it into the river and hope for the best. She carefully placed it in the stream, positioned it safely, and even had his sister, Miriam, keep watch as it floated along.

Now, I like to imagine her backstory. Maybe her dad built fishing boats while she helped take care of her siblings, learning how to work with her hands. Maybe she saw fishermen hide their boats in the reeds to keep them safe from crocodiles in these rivers. The Scriptures don't spell this part out, but somewhere along the way, I feel she learned these skills and used them at just the right moment.

Three months after Moses was born, that moment came. She stepped up, built her little boat, waterproofed it, and placed it strategically in the reeds to protect him. That day, she met her calling head-on. And look at what came from her courage. Her baby boy grew up to change the course of history.

Sometimes, it's easy to feel like our lives are just plain ordinary, especially when we scroll through social media and see everyone else's highlight reel. Someone's launching a business, traveling the world, or hitting milestones we can only dream of. Meanwhile, we're over here just trying to keep up with the day-to-day. It can feel like what we're doing doesn't matter, like we're stuck in the background while everyone else is out there changing the world.

> **WHAT FEELS ORDINARY NOW MIGHT JUST BE THE FOUNDATION FOR SOMETHING EXTRAORDINARY LATER.**

But here's the thing: just like Moses's mom, God is working behind the scenes in ways we can't always see. She wasn't out there making headlines. She was weaving a basket and trusting that what she was doing in the moment was enough. It was God, the Builder of All Things, who intentionally equipped Moses's mom through her life experiences, preparing her for that pivotal moment. He worked through her ordinary actions, using them as part of His greater plan to set Moses on a path and stream to accomplish extraordinary things.

I truly believe God positions us the same way. Even when life feels routine or unimportant, He's equipping us for something great. Those random events, the quiet nudges, the streams we find ourselves floating down, they're not just coincidences. They're part of a larger plan. They're like whispers of destiny, gently steering us toward a purpose we might not fully understand yet.

So, the next time you feel like your life isn't measuring up to what you see online, remember this: what feels ordinary now might just be the foundation for something extraordinary later. Trust the process. God's at work, even when it doesn't look like it.

Jeremiah 1:5 says, "Before I formed you in the womb I knew you." This verse hits deep when you think about Moses. His story shows how God's plan starts long before we even exist. God knew Moses before he was born, just as He knew each of us. That basket floating down the Nile wasn't random; it was all part of a purpose bigger than anyone could see. As the basket floated down the river, it carried more than just a baby. It held the hopes, prayers, and faith of a mother and the beginning of an answer to the cries of a nation. The Israelites were trapped in brutal slavery under Pharaoh, crying out for freedom and looking for a sign that God hadn't forgotten them. They needed a savior, and God chose Moses. He wasn't perfect, but he was called. Through him, God brought plagues to Pharaoh, parted the Red Sea, and set His people free, proving He still had a plan. That basket was the start of it all.

MY BASKET IN THE STREAM

Looking back, I can clearly see the moments in my life that felt like a basket floating down a stream, guiding me toward something I didn't fully understand at the time. There are moments in my story, my life, that I want to share. Ones that show how I've seen God saving me, shaping and preparing me for my calling. Like standing at that metaphorical door with the sign that reads, "You are called for this."

I've had those crossroads and intersections too—moments where everything clicked—and I realized all the challenges and detours weren't random. They were pieces of a bigger plan, preparing me for what was ahead. It's in those moments that I now recognize I was stepping into a purpose that had been woven into my life all along.

My mom's journey has always reminded me of how God works behind the scenes, weaving everything together for a greater purpose, even when we don't realize it. Born in Peoria, Illinois, in the 1950s, her family eventually moved to Cheyenne, Wyoming, near a military base where her dad, my grandpa, was serving. She was just a kid, around eight or nine years old when she fell in love with the magic of the Mickey Mouse Club. In the early 1960s, seeing song and dance brought to life on television like never before must have been incredible. For her, it was more than just entertainment; it sparked something creative inside her, a passion for performance and storytelling.

In just a short time, she took that spark and turned it into something bigger. At just nine years old, she wrote, directed, and staged her first play, pulling in her siblings as cast members. As an early entrepreneur, she even charged the neighborhood kids a nickel to watch. Looking back now, that small play feels like the first step in a much bigger story God was writing for her life.

As she grew older, her dreams grew too. Right after high school, she packed her bags and moved to California, chasing visions of dancing and acting. But after a few months, she realized that wasn't the path for her. By Christmas, she was back home in Peoria, drawn by the pull of family and something deeper she couldn't quite name yet. It was soon after that she met my dad at the restaurant he managed. He hired her as a waitress, and not long after, I came into the picture.

But her journey had just begun. God immediately became the defining thread of her life. She discovered this alongside my grandma, Bonnie, while attending women's meetings together. Those meetings changed everything for both of them. Together, they started serving in prison ministries, bringing hope and encouragement to people who needed it most. It was in those moments praying with inmates and speaking life into dark places that she began to understand the power of her faith and the role music could play in it.

That realization led her to buy her first guitar. She didn't have lessons or a teacher. Just a chord book and a lot of determination. Slowly, chord by chord, she taught herself to play. And when she sang, it wasn't just music—it was her heart pouring out, sharing the love and faith she had found. She didn't just sing songs; she shared her story and her hope with anyone who would listen.

It's like her whole life was leading to something bigger, tying pieces together for a purpose she couldn't yet see. At three years old, just months before our first house fire, I remember her playing the guitar and singing to me. I didn't understand it at the time, but I felt it. Her voice was soft, filled with something I didn't have the words for yet. But now, looking back, I understand. It was her faith. Her faith was like the thread that connected everything—her childhood dreams, her struggles, her love for Jesus, and her role as a mother.

And just like Moses's mom placed him in the basket, trusting God with the outcome, my mom was laying the foundation for something bigger than herself—something she couldn't fully see—but she trusted that God was leading her. That's the beauty of her story. It wasn't just hers; it was mine too. And it was all part of His plan.

All of it. Every moment, every choice, every struggle led to the day she played the guitar for me. I can still hear it. She sang about Jesus, but not like He was some distant figure or idea. She sang like He was someone she knew, someone who had walked with her through every step of her life. I felt her love for this Jesus she was singing about, and somehow, it stirred something in me, even at three years old.

I asked her, "Who is Jesus?" And she told me. She told me like you'd tell someone about a friend who changed your life. She spoke about Him with this kind of peace, like knowing Him had given her a place to rest, even when life wasn't easy. That day, something clicked for me. I didn't have all the answers, but as a three-year-old boy, I believed. I fell in love with Jesus.

Looking back now, I see what I couldn't then, how every moment of her life, every choice she made, and every chord she played, was building up to that moment. Not just for her, but for me too. A few months later, our world turned upside down. We had a devastating house fire. My nine-month-old brother suffered third-degree burns, and I had a near-death experience. On the way to the hospital, my heart stopped from smoke inhalation. I had an experience with Jesus who I believe brought me back. I was revived to life, physically and spiritually. In that moment, I experienced His presence in a way that changed me forever. That encounter with Him has been the guiding light for every step I've taken ever since.

I know for some, the idea of faith can feel foreign, even uncomfortable. Maybe it has hurt you, or maybe you've never really thought about it before. But what I saw in my mom wasn't some religion; it was a straight-up relationship. It was real, and it shaped everything she did. And in that moment, through her music, it became real for me too.

Her legacy didn't end with me. It launched me. She unknowingly laid the foundation for my journey, modeling what it looked like to trust in something bigger, even when the path wasn't clear. My "basket," though, looked different. While hers was woven with music and storytelling, mine was shaped in ways I couldn't yet understand. It wasn't until high school that I began to feel the weight of responsibility and the pull toward something greater. At the time, I didn't know what God was doing, but looking back, I can see how those early moments were preparing me for my own calling. A journey where faith and purpose would lead me into the life God had been shaping for me all along.

HARMONY AND FLOW

Starting high school back in 1994, I remember the blend of excitement and apprehension I felt transitioning from middle school. When I think back on those years, I realize that football didn't initially catch my interest. I grew up with a love for basketball and felt at home dribbling and shooting hoops wherever I went. Football, on the other hand, was a whole different ball game (pun intended). I was unfamiliar with the game, its positions, and the physical intensity involved. Honestly, I wasn't too cool with getting roughed up at the time. To me, football didn't have the swag basketball did, and it was more of a barbaric sport. My mom, who was working as a choreographer at my high school, strongly encouraged me to join the team to get socially engaged early on in the year.

Following my mom's advice, I found myself at the football sign-up table even before the school year officially began. At 6' 2", I stood out as one of the taller and more athletic kids around. So, the coaches decided to slot me in as a defensive end. I had no idea what the position entailed, but I embraced the challenge, diving headfirst into the nasty conditioning sessions of Hell Week.

As I headed into my first freshman football game, I can't remember much about preparing for the game; I'm sure my head was elsewhere, just there in body but not spirit. I do recall the very first play of the game, though. I wasn't well seasoned to get into a specific defensive stance or technique, but I should have been squatting down. I was standing tall, just watching the play. In the game's first play, the opposing team's quarterback dropped back and attempted a pass over me. I found myself frozen in place, not quite sure what to do. But instinct kicked in—I leaped up and snagged the ball, and the sideline erupted into cheers and screams, urging me to run. And I ran, my legs moving in a way that seemed tailor-made for a tailback or running back. Before I knew it, I had juked my way down the field to score a touchdown.

After this unexpected run, my freshman coach approached me and said, "Son, I had no idea you had that kind of speed in you." It might sound like your typical football tale—nothing too extraordinary—but that moment shifted something for me. They decided to slot me in as the starting running back for the remainder of the game and the year, and I felt like I genuinely blossomed in that role. It was a year filled with learning and gaining confidence in the position. I started to comprehend that I no longer feared taking a hit when the ball was in my hands. I began to anticipate how my feet would move, setting the stage for what was to come in my football journey.

During my sophomore year on the varsity team, the varsity coach didn't really take note of my running abilities as a freshman, but he definitely tracked that I was a tall fella. So, similar to my freshman year, he slotted me in as a defensive end on the varsity squad. It was a little different not getting to play with my teammates from last year, the ones who had moved up to the sophomore team now. It was tough not having them by my side on the field anymore. Transitioning to varsity added an extra layer of nerves and discouragement, especially since I wasn't getting much playtime. I was sitting on the bench as a backup defensive end, struggling a bit with the physicality—I just wasn't quite skilled at hitting someone hard on the defensive end.

As we geared up for the first game, coming off a tough 0-9 season the previous year under our varsity coach, who was heading into his second year, there was a mix of nerves and hope. We were optimistic that this season would be different. We had a talented quarterback and a promising group of receivers in the upper class. We were all geared up for what was anticipated to be a standout year. Unfortunately, our starting quarterback suffered a leg injury in the opening game of the season, diminishing our hopes for any wins that year. Things weren't exactly clicking as we had hoped. The team seemed to be a bit disconnected, not entirely tuning in to the coach's game plan.

As the seasons went on, with our record standing at 0-6, and as a sophomore not getting any playing time, I wondered if I was even going to play football anymore. I felt this couldn't be my calling. It really started feeling like a waste of time. To compensate for my discouragement, I supported my sophomore teammates by attending their Saturday morning junior varsity games after our Friday night varsity games. At halftime of one of the JV games, I casually tossed and caught the football with some varsity friends. Little did I know, I was launching the ball an impressive seventy yards. Quite the feat for a high school kid. I suddenly saw my varsity coach sprint onto the field, and for a split second, I thought I was in trouble for playing on the field during the halftime part of the game.

Surprisingly, he said, "Hey, son, toss that ball again."

I had no choice but to throw it again, sending the ball flying another seventy yards with the help of a favorable wind. That's when he dropped the bombshell: I was suiting up as the new quarterback for the upcoming Friday varsity game.

I'll never forget that intense wave of emotions—I don't think I've ever felt so scared in my life. When my friends approached me with what appeared to be exciting news, all I could sense was straight fear. I was literally considering quitting before that Friday game, but now I was the quarterback? Once I got home, I found myself battling nerves, struggling to find the confidence to believe in myself and what I was capable of. Thoughts of still quitting heavily crept into my mind, and that feeling lingered, refusing to budge. While most athletes fantasize about this type of opportunity, I wanted to run away from it entirely.

But then, something started to stir deep inside me. It was like a whisper I couldn't ignore. It reminded me of the way Steve Jobs once described that gut feeling, that unshakable sense that he was meant to do what he was doing. For him, it was building Apple. For me? It was stepping up to play quarterback. It wasn't loud or obvious. It wasn't some booming voice from the heavens. It was subtle. It was like a quiet seed of faith planted right in the middle of all my fear. I couldn't fully explain it, but it felt like God was telling me, *You're here for this. Trust Me.*

That seed of belief, though small, began to grow. It was enough to keep me from walking away. Enough to hold me in place and to think that maybe, just maybe, I wasn't running toward failure. Maybe I was running toward something greater.

As the week rolled on, my top priority was wrapping my head around the plays and mastering the art of handing off the ball. I couldn't help but feel like someone was watching my back, making sure things fell into place, even the little things.

My close friends came up with a creative way to help me out. They handed me a controller and got me playing Madden '94 on the Super Nintendo. At first, it just felt like a game, but it turned out to be surprisingly educational. Looking back, it's almost like something bigger was at work, using something so simple to teach me lessons and prepare me in ways I never saw coming. Slowly but surely, I started to piece together some critical aspects of the game. While I still had a ways to go in truly grasping the ins and outs of football, those moments of connecting the dots felt like a step in the right direction.

The turning point came on that unforgettable Thursday night, the night before the big game. It was late, and my parents were already sound asleep. I heard a knock at the door, and I was caught off guard. Who could be visiting at this hour on a weeknight?

I opened the door and stood there, stunned. It was the star junior wide receiver, standing on my doorstep. I invited him in, and he walked in with a stack of videotapes. I couldn't believe what was happening.

He didn't waste any time. He told me how he saw something in me that I couldn't see in myself. He said I was the answer to his prayers, his hope of making it to the next level. Hearing those words from someone like him—someone I admired—was overwhelming. He genuinely believed in me, and that belief sparked something inside me.

In that quiet, late-night conversation, he helped me find a confidence I didn't know I had. Without him showing up that night, I'm certain I would have let the fear win, closing the door on a chance that would change everything. But because of him, I decided to take the shot, to believe in myself, even if just for a moment.

As the Friday Night Lights game approached, it dawned on me that we were going up against one of the top teams in the state. A team that had top ranking and talent in the state of Illinois, including an all-state quarterback and top-tier wide receivers from Pekin High School who were having a standout season and both Top Division 1 Recruits. This was the opposite of our situation. We were coming off a winless season from the year before and were sitting at 0-6, putting us on a challenging fifteen-game losing streak as we prepared to face off against one of the best teams in the state.

I was just a sixteen-year-old kid on the bus headed to my home field, feeling like I was about to be a huge embarrassment to our school. I can recall the weight of it to this day. It's humbling to admit, but I wanted to straight up cry.

As we were getting warmed up on the field, the skies suddenly opened up, and it started pouring down rain and would continue raining for the rest of the night. Seeking a dry area in the locker room, I made a straight line for the bathroom and found myself almost throwing up due to a case of nerves. Although I was feeling unwell, my teammates were still looking to me as their new leader for guidance and support, pushing me into an unexpected leadership position. It was a role I wasn't accustomed to, apart from being the older sibling to my two brothers and sister.

The pressure mounted as I struggled with the fear of failure. My main goal wasn't about personal success; it was about ensuring the happiness and triumph of my teammates. The last thing I wanted was to disappoint anyone counting on me. The feeling of embarrassment if I let them down was so intense.

Skipping ahead to the game, the coach mainly relied on handing off the ball to get through my debut. However, I attempted eleven passes, completing seven with a high success rate. I came close to reaching 300 passing yards and even managed to toss two touchdowns with zero interceptions despite our loss to Pekin High School by just two points. Yes, two points to one of the best teams in the state. The morning after the game, I couldn't help but feel relief that it was all over. I found myself dreading the thought of going through it all again.

Then, that same Saturday morning, October 7, 1995, I received some unexpected news—my name had been published in the *Peoria Journal Star*. In the 1990s, getting featured in the local newspaper was a big deal. With a mix of excitement and nerves, I eagerly flipped open the paper to read an article highlighting the new kid with a quarterback efficiency rating of 254—the highest in the state. It turned out that my performance had landed me in the top spot in quarterback rating in the entire state of Illinois, and I was the only sophomore on that list.

Suddenly, not only my school and coaches but the whole city was buzzing about this newcomer on the 0-6 team and how the team had only lost to the top-rated team in the state by two points. While it was exciting, the newfound attention also piled on the pressure. I didn't even know how it was possible, as I only passed the ball eleven times.

Moving on to our next game in my coach's second year and my second game, we were up against LaSalle-Peru High School. What stands out vividly is that we secured our first victory. The memory of our coach fainting in excitement on the sidelines after our win still sticks with me. An ambulance had to be called, but thankfully, it was just a case of overwhelming joy. Finally tasting victory meant so much to him. To top it off, we managed to clinch another win in the final game of the season, wrapping up with a two-game winning streak as we headed into my junior year—just to give you a bit of closure.

I would love to share more about my football journey, but there is a greater lesson in what I have shared, aside from how fun it is to reminisce about those feelings. It wasn't about football at all. It was about the beginning stages of God's calling on my life. I thought it was important to share my emotions along the way as I battled these feelings and questioned where God had positioned me. I almost ran away from the door inscribed with the words, "You are called for this." I almost didn't enter the stream God had designed for me. I did go on to play college football, but not at the NFL level, as God had other plans for me to be a quarterback in the business marketplace.

Those years as a quarterback shaped me in ways I never would have imagined. It wasn't just about the wins, the stats, or the Friday night lights. It was about learning how to lead with heart. Football taught me how to see my team, not just as players, but as people. I carried their struggles, their triumphs, their pain, and their hopes. I felt every obstacle we faced together. That empathy became my anchor, and it stuck with me long after I left the field.

> **IT'S NOT ALWAYS ABOUT SOLELY RELYING ON OUR EMOTIONS; PERHAPS IT'S ABOUT RECOGNIZING THE HARMONY AND FLOW OF LIFE THAT GOD IS LAYING OUT FOR US.**

When I moved into construction, I learned the same lessons, just in a different setting. I saw the hard hats and calloused hands, but I also saw the people behind them. I learned to lead with care, to listen, to meet people where they were. And now, in the executive business world, I realize that same quarterback mentality is what drives me. It's about more than strategy or success; it's about understanding that every person on the team matters. God used those years on the field to lay the foundation for something much bigger. Football wasn't just a chapter; it was a training ground for the calling He had waiting for me. And now, I get to carry that same spirit into everything I do.

There are stories in everyone's life that invite us to see our situations from a fresh perspective. It's not always about solely relying on our emotions; perhaps it's about recognizing the **harmony and flow** of life that God is laying out for us. Looking back, I realize that if I had trusted only my feelings of fear, I might have given up on football prematurely and missed out on the leaps of faith necessary to keep me aligned with God's plan and stream for my life.

YOU WERE CHOSEN FOR THIS

Looking at the stream God built in my life, I notice the parallels in how He prepared me for both leadership and administration. With hindsight, I've come to see that being the quarterback for our football team wasn't just about the game; it was God's way of providing me with the leadership skills I'd need for what He had in store for me next.

After playing college football for a year, I joined the Navy, became a squad leader in boot camp, and received the Navy's most prestigious boot camp leader award, "Lone Sailor." Right after boot camp, I headed to military A school in Mississippi for administration training. I worked hard and finished in the top three of my class. Back then, the system was simple: the higher your rank in the class, the earlier you got to pick your orders. The top spot went first, and so on. There were plenty of spots in San Diego and Virginia, about twenty each. But only *one* spot for Japan and *one* for Hawai'i.

I'll never forget sitting there as the first guy stood up. In front of the whole class, he confidently chose Japan for his next four years. My heart sank a little, thinking, *There goes my shot at something extraordinary.* When it was the second guy's turn, I started to settle in my mind for San Diego, convincing myself it wouldn't be so bad. But then, almost instinctively, I started praying, right there, in my chair. *Lord, let me get*

Hawai'i. If You've got something bigger for me, if there's something You're calling me to, let this be it.

It's like God planted a desire in my heart for this place. Hawai'i had always felt like a dreamland to a kid from Illinois. It didn't seem real, like it couldn't ever actually happen. But I kept praying. The second guy stood up, glanced back at me, and said, "You owe me a six-pack, bro." Then he turned to the teacher and said, "I'm picking Virginia. I really want Hawai'i, but my family is in Virginia, so it makes more sense."

I couldn't believe it. I jumped up, like a kid who just won the lottery. I picked Hawai'i without hesitation. My classmates in the room started clapping with excitement for me. They knew a little of my story and how much this meant. And at that moment, I knew it wasn't luck. God was opening a door. Hawai'i wasn't just a place for me; it was the start of something so much bigger.

My mom and I still laugh about the name of the ship I was assigned to in Pearl Harbor, Hawai'i, called the USS *Chosin*. She loves to say, "You were *chosen* for Hawai'i," and honestly, it felt that way. After serving during 9/11 and the Freedom Iraqi War, I returned to Illinois feeling a little lost, unsure of my next steps. I found myself back at church with my mom, praying quietly for direction. That's when a man approached me, looked me over, and said, "You look like a strong young man. Looking for work?" His voice reminded me of my football coaches, pushing me to step up when I wasn't sure I could.

He introduced me to a company called Legacy, and that's where my carpentry journey began. Six months in, I was leading and quarterbacking a fifteen-man crew, constructing modular prefab homes. It was my first real taste of leadership outside the military, and it felt like life was starting to make sense. After a year, life came full circle when I moved back to Hawai'i with Tiffany, where I joined the Carpenters Union to continue my education.

During my carpentry apprenticeship, I had a setback. I got injured and was out of work for three months. It was discouraging, but then something unexpected happened. While I was injured, the owner of Summit Construction, a multimillion-dollar company I had been working for, personally reached out to me. He had noticed my military background as a personnelman (PN) and asked if I could help the project managers who were overwhelmed in the office.

Within a month, I wasn't just assisting; I had stepped into a full project manager role. I worked directly with the VP of operations, learning how to estimate and manage multimillion-dollar projects. It was intense, but as I reflected on those moments, something clicked.

> **LISTEN TO THE WHISPERS OF YOUR LIFE WHEN THEY NUDGE YOU TOWARD SOMETHING BIGGER.**

From quarterbacking on the football field to serving in the Navy and now managing construction teams, every chapter of my life had been preparing me for this. Each experience felt like another piece of a puzzle, falling into place at just the right time. Looking back, I see how life's whispers had guided me all along, pulling me closer to the purpose I was created for. Now, as a husband, father, papa, business owner, and entrepreneur, I know without a doubt—I was chosen for this. Looking back on this journey makes me wonder how one can recognize one's true calling early and be in tune enough to stay on its path. One of the most exciting experiences is when you sense that moment of connection and realization, understanding that you are meant to do what you're doing.

As you read this, you might not feel like you're standing before some grand, metaphorical door with your life purpose written on it. And that's okay. Not everyone gets a lightning-bolt moment. For some, purpose feels like a whisper carried on the wind, gently steering you when you're not even sure where you're headed sometimes. But here's what I've learned: those whispers matter. The small nudges, gut feelings, and even the setbacks—they're all part of something bigger. Maybe you don't believe in a God orchestrating your story, and that's okay. But you can't deny that life has a way of weaving together moments, decisions, and experiences into something that just *feels* like it was meant to be.

So, here's my challenge: Pay Attention.

Pay attention to the things that light you up, even if they terrify you. Listen to the whispers of your life when they nudge you toward something bigger. Maybe it's stepping up at work, pursuing a passion you've buried, or simply saying yes to an opportunity that scares you. Trust the process. Even when the wind feels unpredictable, it's carrying you somewhere. Somewhere worth stepping into.

> **SONG PAIRING:** "I'll Find You" by Lecrae feat. Tori Kelly
> *All Things Work Together* (Album)[12]

---

12 Lecrae, vocalist, "I'll Find You" by Natalie Sims, Sasha Sloan, et al., released June 9, 2017, track 11 on *All Things Work Together,* Reach Records.

CHAPTER 5

THE SWIM:
The 153 Season

Do All You Know to Do, and Let God Do the Rest

> *"The horse is made ready for the day of battle, but victory rests with the LORD."*
> —Proverbs 21:31

PREPARING THE FIELD

Let me take you back to 2003, during the early days of Operation Iraqi Freedom. I was stationed on a Navy warship in the middle of the Persian Gulf, serving as the communication link between the central command and the captain of the ship. When the alarm for general quarters would go off, sometimes at 2 a.m., I'd take my position, headset on, with adrenaline pumping. In my call of duty, every call I relayed carried serious weight. We never knew if it was just another drill or if we were heading straight into a life-or-death situation.

We were all trained to prepare for the worst yet trust that everything we'd done would hold under that stress and pressure.

I'll never forget the first time we went head-to-head with an Iraqi warship. All I could think was, *If they fire a missile at us, there's nothing we can do but take the hit and pray we survive.*

Out there in the endless ocean, at the mercy of war, where control feels like a distant memory, I held tight to trusting in this scripture: "The horse is made ready for the day of battle, but victory rests with the LORD" (Proverbs 21:31).

That verse became my anchor. It encouraged me to stay prepared like my life depended on it—because it did. But I knew the ultimate outcome wasn't in my hands; it was in God's. It gave me peace in the chaos, a reminder that while I was called to do my part, He was the one writing the final chapter.

Preparing for battle wasn't just about mental readiness; it was about a spirit of diligence. I saw it then, and I see it now in everything I do, whether it's growing a business, leading my family, or navigating life's challenges. The scripture reminds me that while preparation is our responsibility, victory isn't ours to control. That's in the hand of the Builder of All Things Himself.

Picture this: a warrior tending to his horse, tightening every strap, sharpening every blade, checking provisions, and planning for every possible scenario. That was us on the ship. That was me running my business. And maybe, in your own way, that's you right now. We prepare like it all depends on us because it's our duty to give our best. But at the same time, we try to obtain the victory ourselves.

It's not just about doing the work; it's about doing it with purpose. If we can establish the perspective of faith that the destination is already determined, our role then is to steward what we've been given. Whether you believe in God or not, there's power in recognizing that the weight of victory isn't on our shoulders alone. It's freeing, and it gives our every effort a deeper meaning.

And that's when it all clicked for me. There was someone else in this fight alongside me, someone I hadn't fully recognized until that moment. The Partner I never knew I had. He wasn't just watching from the sidelines; He'd been laying out streams of opportunity all along, weaving them seamlessly into my path. But this is the truth that stopped me in my tracks: those opportunities weren't unlocked by luck or coincidence. They were the result of obedience and diligence. Showing up, doing the work, and trusting that there was a bigger plan in motion. The victories that I used to think were out of reach? They were already in the works, just waiting for my actions of faithfulness to align with His perfect timing.

Here is a truth that is undeniable: diligence and preparation can open doors, but there's always that element of timing and opportunity we just can't control. This is a great place to start and think about those moments when things fell into place in ways you couldn't have planned or predicted. Coincidence? Or maybe, just maybe, there's a Partner behind the scenes, aligning things for you. You don't need all the answers to take the first step. Start with gratitude. Look for those moments when opportunity meets your effort. And if you're up for it, ask yourself this simple question: *What if there's more to this than I can see?* No need to overthink it, just let it be an honest starting point to explore what's already at work in your life.

Now, let's be real. If you're running a business without integrity, cutting corners, doing illegal things to get ahead, cheating people, stealing, or anything that dishonors the God I'm referring to, any success you think you've achieved? That didn't come from Him. That's all on you, and it's yours to carry. Trust me, that's a burden you don't want to bear alone.

But here's where everything shifts. Just because you've taken some wrong turns doesn't mean it's game over. You can choose to start the path of diligence and obedience right now and let the Builder of All Things guide you back. It's never too late to realign yourself with integrity and purpose. Maybe you've been making choices that don't sit right with your soul. That stops today. The moment you decide to change course and do things the right way, you're not alone in this journey. He's right there beside you, ready to turn your renewed commitment into victories you can't even imagine. So why not take that step? Why not see what happens when you let the ultimate Partner lead the way?

There's a scene in the movie *Facing the Giants* that hit me hard, especially with my football background. The coach in the movie is going through a rough time. The team is losing, his job is on the line, his players are falling apart, and he's being crushed by the weight of personal struggles at home. Bills are stacking up, and he and his wife are facing the heartbreak of infertility. He's in a place many of us have been, doing all he can and still feeling like it's not enough.

Then, out of nowhere, the school pastor walks into his office and shares this story about two farmers who both prayed for rain. But only one of them went out and prepared his fields to receive it. When the rain finally came, only one was ready to reap the harvest.[13]

> **FAITH WITHOUT ACTION IS DEAD, BUT ACTION WITHOUT FAITH MISSES THE WHOLE POINT.**

That story reminds me of a truth I've lived out many times, on the field, in business, and in life. There's a part we're called to play, doing everything we know to do. That farmer didn't just sit around hoping for rain; he got to work. And that's what we've done in every season. Building, preparing, and stewarding what we've been given, even when it felt like we were waiting on something bigger. But here's the key: once we've done all we can, that's when we step back and let the Builder of All Things do the rest. Whether it's a coach praying for his team, a farmer waiting for rain, or a business owner trusting his sales for growth, the principle is the same. Faith without action is dead, but action without faith misses the whole point. You've got to do the work and trust the One who brings the rain.

---

[13] Alex Kendrick, *Facing the Giants* (September 29, 2006; Albany, GA: Kendrick Brothers).

RIGHT SIDE OF THE BOAT

From 2017 to 2018, our business really started to take off. We had to grow the office and bring on folks like project managers, lead coordinators, and office assistants to keep up. Opportunities looked promising, so we focused on tightening our processes to make sure nothing slipped through the cracks. As we sensed the growth ahead, we knew preparation was key.

But then, in 2019, we hit a milestone that changed everything. We landed our first high-end luxury home remodel contract, worth two million dollars. It was a moment we had worked so hard for, but let me tell you, it wasn't just about the effort we put in. There's an old saying, "Luck is when preparation meets opportunity," but I'd rephrase it like this: "God's favor is when your diligence aligns with your purpose."

Here's what that means: we have a part to play. It's on us to show up, put in the work, and give our very best. But at some point, you realize there are things in life that you just can't control—like the right doors opening or the right opportunities finding their way to you. That's where God comes in. When your hard work aligns with His plan for your life, something incredible happens. It's not luck; it's His favor. You start to see that while you're paddling as hard as you can, He's the one guiding the current of your life. That's the beauty of it. Doing everything in your power while trusting Him to carry you the rest of the way.

When we finally got the permit for that first luxury project, it felt like everything was falling into place. It was February 2020, and our team was ready to go. We'd spent months preparing, putting all the pieces together for what was shaping up to be a dream project with a dream client. We were doing everything we knew we had to do. Geared up, motivated, and riding this wave of momentum that felt unstoppable.

But then, just one month later, in March 2020, the entire world changed. Most of you know what it was like, but let me set the scene for how it impacted my business.

COVID-19 wasn't just a sickness; it was a global pandemic that caused everything to shut down. Schools, businesses, airports—everything just stopped. There was no roadmap, no way to predict what was coming. Fear spread faster than the virus itself, and the world went into lockdown. People were told to stay home. Businesses closed their doors. Millions of jobs disappeared overnight, and life as we knew it was turned upside down.

For us, it was devastating. We had every single one of our projects come to a halt and shut down. I still remember those calls—subcontractors canceling schedules, employees too scared to come to work, and clients putting projects on hold indefinitely. Our job sites became ghost towns. Those initial first few weeks were filled with so much fear and uncertainty that no one knew how to move forward. The momentum we'd been building felt like it had vanished, and suddenly, we were left asking, "What now?" How were we supposed to navigate a situation like this, keep our projects going, pay our bills, and lead our team? It felt like standing in the middle of a storm, looking at the waves crashing down, and not knowing which way to turn.

I know what it's like day in and day out. You're running your business, giving it everything you've got. Long nights, early mornings, pouring your energy and heart into it. You're doing all the things they tell you to do, following the playbook, grinding harder than anyone else. But then there are those seasons that are out of your control, and the results just aren't there. Every strategy, every plan, every ounce of effort feels like it's hitting a brick wall.

You might ask yourself, *Am I meant to do this, and am I meant to do this right now? What am I missing? Did I overlook something? Is all this even worth it anymore?* That doubt creeps in, and it's heavy. It makes you question everything. It's that moment when the grind starts to feel more like quicksand, pulling you down no matter how hard you fight to climb out.

That's exactly how it felt when COVID-19 hit. One day, you're out there building your dream business, your plans, your future, and then suddenly, the world stops, literally. Everything you thought you could count on gets flipped upside down. Contracts canceled. Doors closed. Clients vanished. If you're anything like me, you probably had moments where you looked around and thought, *How am I supposed to keep going?*

The truth is, for a lot of us, COVID-19 didn't just test our businesses; it tested us. It forced us to ask the hard questions: *What am I really building? Am I ready for what's coming next? Do I have the grind to weather this storm? Do I have the humility to adapt?* It was a season of empty nets, and for many of us, it felt like the hits just kept coming.

But here's the thing. That's also where diligence and preparation meet opportunity. COVID-19 was brutal, no question, but it also taught us something: sometimes, the biggest breakthroughs come right after you've pushed through the hardest nights.

For those of you who didn't make it through COVID-19 with your business, let me be clear—I'm not saying you did anything wrong. Sometimes, a chapter ends because its time has run its course. But don't let that stop you. This could be the moment for your next chapter, the spark for a new idea, or the beginning of something even greater waiting to bloom.

But, if you're still feeling that weight, I get it. I've been there. But let me tell you something; that season isn't where the story ends. If you're still showing up, still preparing, still learning, and still adjusting, then you're positioning yourself for when the tide changes. And when it does, all that hard work and hustle will meet the moment. Your nets might feel empty now, but the opportunity is coming. Stay ready.

Let me tell you about a group of fishermen who had a night just like the one I described earlier. Their story is in the Scriptures, found in John 21—a mirror of what we talked about in chapter 2. These weren't amateurs; these guys were the real deal. Fishing was their livelihood, their expertise, their daily grind. But after an entire night of hard work, their nets were empty. No fish, no payday, no answers. Sound familiar?

> *"I'm going out to fish," Simon Peter told them, and they said, "We'll go with you." So they went out and got into the boat, but that night they caught nothing.*
> —John 21:3

But here's where it gets interesting. This time, they knew Jesus. They'd already walked with Him, gone through His apprenticeship. They did everything they knew how to do, used every method in the book, every trick of the trade, but still came up short. Why?

I believe Jesus was showing them one last lesson, a final teaching moment to prepare them for their next step—to graduate into what they were called to do. Because they didn't have Jesus at that moment, in the boat, as their source of power. It's like having all the latest construction power tools; you can own the best of the best, but they're close to useless if you don't have a power source to plug them into.

> **IT'S NOT ABOUT JUST CHASING ANY OPPORTUNITY; IT'S ABOUT CHOOSING THE ONES THAT ACTUALLY ALIGN WITH SOMETHING GREATER.**

Sometimes, we lean so hard on our own skills and hustle that we forget, without connecting to the true source of power, that our best efforts might still fall short. The fisherman learned that the hard way. All night, they worked, doing everything they knew how to do, but their nets stayed empty. It wasn't until they listened to Jesus, followed His direction, and cast their nets that everything changed. Their nets overflowed with fish, more than they could handle. It wasn't just about their effort. It was about plugging into the power only He provides.

Sure, you can run your business on your own and probably see some success, but that's not the issue. If you treat your work like a quick transaction, expecting fast results without any real purpose behind it, you're missing the bigger picture. The difference is this: it's not about just chasing any opportunity; it's about choosing the ones that actually align with something greater. Something that not only grows your business but fulfills your purpose.

Sure, those fishermen were out there, trying to catch enough for dinner or maybe stock up for the week. But let's be real—it wasn't just about having a profitable afternoon. Deep down, they were chasing something more. They wanted to be part of something bigger, something that mattered. They craved purpose, a legacy. They wanted to be used for something greater than just making ends meet. Especially after walking with Jesus for three years.

Obedience and diligence go together like a hammer and nail. Those fishermen weren't lazy. They were experts. Fishing wasn't a hobby for them; it was their life. They knew the water, the nets, the techniques, and the best days, nights, and locations for a successful catch. They were diligent, working tirelessly through the night. But sometimes, diligence alone isn't enough. As the sun came up, they saw this Guy standing on the shore:

Early in the morning, Jesus stood on the shore, but the disciples did not realize that it was Jesus.

> He called out to them, "Friends, haven't you any fish?"
>
> "No," they answered.
>
> He said, "Throw your net on the right side of the boat and you will find some." When they did, they were unable to haul the net in because of the large number of fish. —John 21:4-6

Now, let's be real. I can imagine their reaction. The right side? Seriously? They'd been out there all night, throwing that net over and over, trying everything they knew. What difference was a few feet gonna make? But here's the thing—they chose to obey, even when it didn't make sense. They cast their net on the right side, just like He said, and boom. Their nets were bursting with fish.

You can have the best tools in the game, but if they're not plugged into the power, they're just dead weight. The second you connect them to power, they come alive. That's when they can actually do what they were made to do. It's the same with us. You can hustle, grind, and push as hard as you want, but if you're not plugged into the power that will fulfill your purpose, you'll never operate the way you were truly designed to.

The Builder of All Things, the One who designed it all, speaks to us in ways we don't always expect—through our highs, through our struggles, and even through people who might just be crossing our path. For someone like you, running a business, this isn't just some feel-good talk. It's real. When you stop relying only on what you know and start tuning into that deeper guidance, you're plugging into a power source that makes a connection with everything you're already doing.

This is where obedience and diligence come together. Look, you've already been putting in the work. But when you add obedience—listening to that nudge that says, *Try it this way*, or *Go in that direction*, or even *Throw on the right side*—that's when things start to change.

The fishermen reached the peak of what diligence really means—doing everything they knew they needed to do. Then came that suggestion from the shore: "Throw your net on the right side." And it hit them. Why would this person even ask? If they didn't listen, if they didn't try, they wouldn't be doing everything they knew how to do. That moment of humility, that decision to act, was their last drop of diligence, the final step that unlocked what was waiting for them.

Don't just keep grinding with the power turned off. Plug in. Tap into that source that takes everything you're doing and gives it purpose. That's how you go from just working hard to truly building something that lasts and is fulfilling.

Even if you're not sure about faith or Jesus, think about it this way: Imagine being in a stream. You can fight the current all you want, but it's not until you trust its guidance and flow with it that you'll reach the destination you were meant for. You don't have to fully understand the water or even believe in it to experience its power.

So maybe it's not just about effort and expertise. Maybe it's about being open to guidance that goes beyond what you can see. The fishermen's story is proof that when diligence meets obedience, especially to a trustworthy source, the results can blow your mind. What if there's more at play than what you can control? What if plugging into that power source changes everything? And that one decision *did* change everything. They cast their net on the other side, and suddenly, it was overflowing. The story even says they caught exactly 153 fish:

> *Jesus said to them, "Bring some of the fish you have just caught." So Simon Peter climbed back into the boat and dragged the net ashore. It was full of large fish, 153, but even with so many the net was not torn.* —John 21:10-11

Here's why that hits home for me and why I think it might be for you too. First off, sometimes the solution isn't about working harder; it's about working differently. Those fishermen didn't catch more fish because they stayed out longer or rowed to another spot. They caught more fish because they were willing to try something new, even when it didn't seem logical. How often do we get stuck in our ways, thinking, *I've already tried everything?* Maybe you haven't. Maybe the breakthrough is just a small shift away.

> **WHEN YOU ALIGN YOUR DILIGENCE WITH HIS TIMING, THAT'S WHEN EVERYTHING FALLS INTO PLACE.**

Second, it's about knowing when to listen. That advice came from someone they didn't even recognize at first. What if they'd brushed him off? What if their pride got in the way? As business owners, we're often the experts in the room, but sometimes the best advice comes from unexpected places—whether it's a team member, a friend, or even a total stranger. The question is, are you open to hearing it? Or are you so set in your ways that you're ready to fight the current and risk slapping all your hard work and effort right in the face?

And finally, timing is everything. Those fishermen weren't messing up; they were just casting their nets at the wrong time, in the wrong spot. Success in business is a lot like that. You can do all the right things and put in all the hard work, but if the timing isn't right, the results just won't be there. But here's the thing: God is always preparing the spot for you, lining up the opportunities, bringing the fish in due time. When His timing clicks, and you're in the right place doing the right things, the results can be better than you ever imagined. It's not just about our effort. It's about trusting that He's setting things up behind the scenes. When you align your diligence with His timing, that's when everything falls into place.

Look, I get it—business can feel like a grind sometimes, and the empty nets can make you question everything. But maybe the answer isn't to throw in the towel. Maybe it's to throw the net on the other side of the boat. Be open to new perspectives. Trust the process. And stay ready for the moment when things start to change. Because when that moment comes, and it will, your nets will be full to capacity. And that is what I like to call the "153 Season."

153 SEASON

For us, at that moment when COVID-19 hit and the world felt like it was crumbling, everything uncertain and fear around every corner, we recognized a peace, a peace knowing that we were actually prepared. Looking back, I could personally see how every moment in the Navy prepared me for this. The drills, the discipline, the readiness for the unknown. It all came rushing back. When every one of our projects froze in place, we didn't fold. We trusted Him and built a battle plan, knowing our strength wasn't just in preparation but in faith. We were ready to throw the net on the other side. We felt that nudge to shift how we were doing things. It was a call to pivot, to trust the flow instead of fighting it, and to lean into the process.

It wasn't easy, but it was clear: don't quit, don't give up. When every one of our ongoing projects came to a halt, we trusted Him and continued to put a battle plan together. We emailed this plan to all our clients, outlining how we could continue working safely and responsibly. The plan included strict safety measures: wearing masks at all times, installing cleaning stations, taking regular breathing breaks to step away and regroup, and adhering to every guideline to protect our team and the community. We emphasized that construction was legally considered essential in Hawai'i, which allowed us to keep moving forward if our clients permitted. We also outlined how we would ensure critical vendors and supply chains were secured, so the projects could continue without interruption.

Out of all the clients we reached out to, only one replied—and it just so happened to be the two-million-dollar high-end luxury project we'd been so excited about. It felt like confirmation, a clear sign that God was making a way where there seemed to be none. Suddenly, we had a fully available team, carpenters, and subcontractors ready to go, and a single, high-stakes project to focus all our energy on. The homeowner, living on the mainland, created the perfect environment for us to work uninterrupted, and we knew this wasn't just luck. It was the Builder of All Things, constructing every detail. We knew the victory was His.

We poured everything we had into this project, pivoting quickly to adapt. We provided extra training for our team, ensuring they understood the new safety measures and could adjust to the unique challenges of the moment. Leveraging technology, we maintained a clear line of communication with the client through our online portal and virtual meetings, ensuring their involvement despite the distance. We had been using video calls and tech tools long before the pandemic, so it felt like we were prepared for this exact moment. While others were scrambling to adjust, our field was ready. It wasn't just about survival; it was about thriving in the midst of the challenge, aligning diligence with faith, and trusting God to carry us through. That project became a testimony to His provision and a reminder that when you're prepared to move in faith, the Builder of All Things always comes through. God's favor was with us because our diligence aligned with our purpose.

We ended up completing the home in record time—six months. This was a huge win for us, considering the world was shut down at the time. The home was later featured on the front covers of the island's most esteemed luxury home magazines with full-story spreads. We received design-build awards nationally and locally.

Following this wave of recognition and achievement, a significant shift occurred. We became the island's trailblazers in embracing innovative practices. During a time when everything felt uncertain, we leaned into innovation like true pioneers. We introduced practices that were ahead of their time like paperless blueprints, iPad programs for the field, and online portals for our clients. These tools didn't just keep us moving forward; they set a new standard. And we didn't stop there. We started sharing what we were doing, passing on these tools to other contractors in our market, raising the bar for everyone.

Momentum kept building. By 2021, we hit a stride that felt almost surreal. Our growth skyrocketed as we made it onto the prestigious Inc. 5000 list of the fastest-growing companies in the nation.[14] Out of thousands of companies, we stood tall as one of the top fifty fastest-growing construction companies nationally. Back home, we were honored in the *Hawaii Business Top 250 Black Book* list and recognized as top executives on the island.[15] On top of that, we were named Hawaii's Best Builder and Best Interior Designer.[16]

But this isn't about a highlight reel of accolades. This book you're holding isn't a step-by-step guide to mountain-high

---

14 "Hawaii Business Top 25 Black Book List," Inc., https://www.inc.com/profile/atn-construction.
15 Cynthia Wessendorf, "Hawai'i's Top 250 Companies 2022: List Now Available Online," HawaiiBusiness Magazine, 6 September, 2022, https://www.hawaiibusiness.com/hawaii-top-250-companies-businesses-2022/#top-250-list-2022
16 Stephanie Nguyen, "2021 Readers' Choice Awards: Builder," *Hawaii Home + Remodeling*, 17 May 2021, https://www.hawaiihomemag.com/2021-readers-choice-awards-builder-2/.

success or some cookie-cutter formula to profits. It's our story, a journey of walking with God, leaning on faith, and learning to see every situation through His lens. That year felt like a season of harvest, yes. Magazine covers, awards, national rankings, a growing team of fifty—it all sounds like triumph, and in many ways, it was. But for me, true success wasn't just in the achievements. It was in the journey, the lessons, and the growth along the way.

And that's why celebrating the victories matters. Not to pat ourselves on the back but to pause and reflect and praise what the Builder of All Things has done. Gratitude isn't just something we owe Him; it's the fuel that keeps us moving forward. Taking time to honor Him and acknowledge how far He's brought us is what sustains the journey. Every milestone, every step forward, serves as a reminder that it's all His. That's worth celebrating. Always.

Let me share something that could change the way you see your work and your life—that concept I'm calling the "153 Season." This isn't just a catchy phrase to throw around. It's about those powerful, life-shifting moments when the Builder of All Things shows up and fills your nets with blessings you can't even contain. It's a season where everything lines up, where your obedience to Him, your faith, and your hard work come together and the miraculous happens right in front of you.

Think about it. They didn't catch 150 fish. Not 155. They caught exactly 153. That number wasn't random. Jesus was precise, deliberate, and intentional about which fish hit those nets. It was the perfect catch—not a single fish too many or too few. The nets didn't break. They were filled to their maximum potential. That's the picture of God's abundance: more than enough, but never too much to handle.

The 153 Season is when God steps in and blesses you in ways that blow your mind. It's not just in business—it's in life, relationships, and purpose. It's that season of incredible fruitfulness when you're flowing in the stream of God's will, letting Him take the lead. It's not about working harder or trying to control everything. It's about aligning your diligence with His direction. That's where the real power is.

Remember, these fishermen were pros. They knew how to fish. They did everything they could on their own, but it wasn't working. Sound familiar? Sometimes, we grind so hard, thinking we've got it all figured out, but we're missing the key ingredient: God's guidance. They didn't experience their 153 Season until they listened to Jesus and cast their net exactly where He told them. That's the beauty of it. It wasn't about their skill; it was about their obedience.

So, if you feel like you've been working all night and have nothing to show for it, maybe it's time to stop relying on your own plans. Maybe it's time to listen for that voice, to trust the One who's been preparing your catch all along. When you do, you might just step into your own 153 Season.

> *"That person is like a tree planted by streams of water, which yields its fruit in season and whose leaf does not wither—whatever they do prospers."*
> —Psalms 1:3

JUMPING IN THE WATER

I want to talk about something that's always been close to my heart: what real leadership looks like to me. This is a message I think every CEO, every leader, needs to hear. When we step into a 153 Season—those moments when blessings are overflowing and everything feels within reach—the condition of our hearts is what matters most. It's not just about what we've gained; it's about how we handle it and who we're honoring in the process.

It's what keeps us grounded, guides our decisions, and determines how we steward the abundance God entrusts to us. And let's not forget who gave us the key to where the fish were—the One who brought them to that exact spot just for us:

Be careful that you do not forget the LORD your God, failing to observe his commands, his laws and his decrees that I am giving you this day. Otherwise, when you eat and are satisfied, when you build fine houses and settle down, and when your herds and flocks grow large and your silver and gold increase and all you have is multiplied, then your heart will become proud, and you will forget the LORD your God. —Deuteronomy 8:11-14

Let's take a moment to really feel the weight of how Peter reacted in his own 153 Season. His net was suddenly filled with fish, a haul so big it could've been life-changing for any fisherman. But Peter didn't get caught up in the abundance, didn't pause to strategize his next big move, and didn't even stop to admire the miracle. The moment he realized it was **Jesus** standing on that shore, he didn't hesitate. Peter jumped straight out of the boat, into the water, and swam to Him. No second-guessing, no distractions. That's leadership. That's the heart of a king.

> **WHEN THE BIG WINS COME, DON'T GET SO BUSY COUNTING THE FISH THAT YOU FORGET WHO FILLED YOUR NETS IN THE FIRST PLACE.**

Peter didn't let the blessings distract him from the Blesser. He knew exactly where the fish had come from, and he wasn't about to waste time focusing on the fish when the source of it all was standing right in front of him. He didn't stop to count the fish or marvel at the catch. He made a beeline to Jesus, the One who made it all possible.

As leaders and business owners, it's so easy to get caught up in the grind. We're wired to focus on the metrics, the growth, the accolades. But true leadership, the kind that reflects the heart of a king, isn't about getting lost in the wins. It's about keeping our eyes on the One who's guiding us. Especially when the nets are full, it's about staying humble, staying grateful, and staying connected to the relationship that fuels it all.

So, as we close this chapter, let's unpack what it means to lead with that kind of heart. Let's not lose sight of the One who brought us here, who opened the doors, who filled the nets.

Because at the end of the day, it's not just about the blessings we receive—it's about how we honor the One who gives them.

> *Then the disciple whom Jesus loved said to Peter, "It is the Lord!" As soon as Simon Peter heard him say, "It is the Lord," he wrapped his outer garment around him (for he had taken it off) and jumped into the water. The other disciples followed in the boat, towing the net full of fish, for they were not far from shore, about a hundred yards. When they landed, they saw a fire of burning coals there with fish on it, and some bread."* —John 21:7-9

So, what does this mean for you as a business owner? It's a reminder that no matter how successful we become in our obedience, our achievements should never overshadow our relationship with the Partner we may not have known we had—the Builder of All Things. When the big wins come, don't get so busy counting the fish that you forget who filled your nets in the first place.

> *"Jesus said to them, 'Come and have breakfast.'"*
> —John 21:12

When the fish come from Him and we're in that 153 Season, He doesn't just send us off with a blessing and say, "Good luck." No, He invites us to sit down and enjoy it *with Him*. He doesn't pour out abundance so we can hoard it, eat alone, or let it sit and rot. Instead, He calls to us, "Come and have breakfast." How incredible is He? Can you picture it? The fire was already burning when the disciples got to shore. He'd already prepared the space, ready to share the moment with them.

That's the heart of the 153 Season. It's not just about the catch, the success, or the blessings; it's about the relationship. It's about sitting with the One who made it all possible, sharing in the moment, and letting Him remind you that He's not just providing; He's present. The greatest part of the 153 Season isn't the fish—it's the fellowship.

Diligence is preparing your net. It's showing up, doing the work, honing your craft, and staying ready, even when you don't see results right away. It's having your tools in place and your heart in the right posture. But obedience? That's throwing your net to the other side when He tells you to, even when it feels pointless or you've been grinding all night with nothing to show for it. It's trusting in guidance that goes beyond what you can see.

Business isn't all sunshine and overflowing nets. It's a mix—seasons of fruitfulness and seasons that test you. Some days, your nets will be full, and other days they'll come up empty. But here's the hope: Jesus is always there, standing on the shore, ready to guide you. He's not distant. He's close, calling out, offering direction that can completely change your outcome if you're willing to listen.

Remember this: your diligence sets the stage, but your obedience brings the breakthrough. So keep preparing, keep listening, and be ready to move when He calls. When you align your efforts with His guidance, that's when nets get filled, hearts overflow, and your purpose becomes something greater than you ever imagined.

153 Season Definition: A season of extraordinary blessing and fruitfulness, inspired by the miraculous catch of 153 fish in John 21. It represents the abundance that comes when you honor God, walk in obedience, and diligently align your efforts with His divine timing. This season is profound not just for its abundance but for its intentionality. God fills your net with "good fish"—precise, purposeful blessings—while keeping out what could harm or weigh you down.

Additional Encouragement: Remember, do all that you know you need to do, and let God do the rest. Trust that God will continue to open doors and place the right tasks in your path. You won't be able to conquer every opportunity that comes your way, and that's okay. Not every opportunity is for you. Pray for God to open the doors that align with your purpose and close those that don't, so you can remain focused and diligent. Let God steer the helm while you faithfully do your part.

> **SONG PAIRING:** "Celebrate More" by Lecrae feat. Hulvey and Andy Mineo
> *Restoration* (The Deluxe Album)[17]

---

[17] Lecrae, vocalist, "Celebrate More," by Andrew Aaron Mineo, Christopher Michael Hulvey, et al., released July 31, 2020, track 20 on *Restoration: The Deluxe Album,* Reach Records.

PART 3
BATTLING ADVERSITY

INTERLUDE

CHALLENGES

The Storm, the Snake, the Smoke

Running a business isn't for those who lack courage. Some days, it feels like you're cruising down the open waters. Sun shining, engine humming, everything clicking just the way you planned. But then, out of nowhere, the sky darkens, the wind picks up, and you're caught in a storm you didn't see coming. Or maybe you notice something slithering in the shadows, and before you know it, you've been bitten by someone you thought you could trust. And then there are those moments when you realize that smoke is clouding your vision; it's rising from your own fires, sparked by your own mistakes.

I would like to challenge and redefine your perspective. When adversity arises, do not look at every challenge as a storm. As we move into the next three chapters, my hope is that we'll learn to assess and sort the challenges we face into one of these three categories: The Storm, the Snake, and the Smoke. When we can identify them clearly, we'll be better equipped to respond in the right way and overcome them with purpose and confidence. The key is figuring out what kind of challenge you're really up against so you can handle it the right way and come out stronger.

Storms in business are those external challenges that are beyond your control and not directly caused by you. But sometimes, these business storms aren't just random gusts trying to knock your company off course. They're actually opportunities in disguise—to learn, to grow, and to sharpen your leadership as a business owner. Embracing these challenges with the right mindset can transform your business and elevate your leadership to new heights.

Then, there's the snake. This one's different because it's personal. The snake isn't the wind or the waves. It's the betrayal that slithers into your life when you least expect it. It's the business partner who stabs you in the back, the competitor who spreads lies about you, or the team member who undermines everything you've built. The snake is deceitful, deliberate, and strikes with precision.

And then there's the smoke. This one's harder to admit because it comes from you. The smoke clouds your judgment, blurs your vision, and makes it hard to see the way forward. But unlike the storm or the snake, the smoke is self-inflicted. It's the result of your own decisions—decisions you wish you could take back.

As you navigate life and business, you're going to face challenges. They're part of the journey. But here's the truth: every challenge is an opportunity. The storm strengthens your resilience. The snake sharpens your discernment. And the smoke humbles you, reminding you to stay grounded and accountable.

Remember, you're the co-captain of your ship, and no matter what comes your way, you don't sail alone. The Builder of All Things is with you in the storm, giving you peace when the waves are high. He protects you from the snake and exposes the lies for what they are. And He helps you clear the smoke, offering grace and a fresh start when you need it most. So, hold steady. The challenges will come, but they don't define you. What defines you is how you respond—how you lead, how you grow, and how you stay anchored in faith. Let's set sail and face these waters together.

CHAPTER 6

THE STORM:
Wake Him Up

Faith Over Fear

> *"The disciples went and woke him, saying, 'Lord, save us! We're going to drown!'"*
> —Matthew 8:25

THE STORM

I grew up as a kid in Illinois, where we had some of the craziest storms you've ever seen. Just a regular rainstorm or thunderstorm sometimes looked like a tornado had blown through by the next morning. My friends and I would grab our bikes and ride around after the storm passed, just to see how many trees and telephone poles had been knocked over, how many houses had been hit. It was like a full-on disaster scene. Uprooted trees blocked the streets, power lines hung low like jungle vines, and entire neighborhoods looked like they had been rearranged by a giant hand. Meanwhile, fire engines and police were trying to keep everyone safe. As kids, we didn't grasp the severity of it all; to us, it was one of the coolest adventures ever. We didn't think about the property damage, the injuries, or the lives lost because of the storm. But all we had to do was look around to appreciate and understand its power.

I've learned something about those Midwest storms I grew up with; they didn't just come out of nowhere. If you paid attention, you could see them coming long before the first raindrop hit. We had this practical little trick based on how light and sound travel. When we'd see a lightning flash, we'd start counting the seconds until we heard the thunder. Each second roughly translated to a mile in distance. The shorter the count, the closer the storm. We'd feel the wind pick up, see the dark clouds rolling in, and know it was time to get ready. We never knew exactly when the storm would hit, but we knew it was coming.

In business, we go through challenges that aren't much different from storms. They give us indicators if we're tuned in. I like to call these the wind, lightning, thunder, and rain of the business world. Maybe it's a subtle shift in your market trends—the wind changing direction. Then comes the first flash of lightning, like when a key competitor unexpectedly launches a revolutionary product that disrupts your business. Perhaps it's a sudden increase in customer complaints—the thunder rolling in. And finally, the first drops of rain hit when these challenges start affecting your bottom line. By recognizing each element of the storm, you can better prepare and respond, ensuring your business not only weathers the storm but also emerges stronger.

If we're wise, we'll recognize these signs early. We'll feel the wind of changing consumer behavior and adjust our sails accordingly. We'll see the lightning of emerging technologies and prepare to adapt. We'll hear the thunder of regulatory changes and get our house in order. By the time the rain starts, we'll be ready—not scrambling for shelter, but navigating confidently through the storm.

The key is not to ignore the signs. Just like counting the seconds between lightning and thunder told us how far away the storm was, paying attention to the indicators in our business can tell us what's coming and how urgent it is. It's about being proactive rather than reactive.

Remember, the storms will come—that's a given. But if we learn to read the signs, we won't just survive them; we'll come out stronger on the other side.

One thing's for sure: a storm is Mother Nature at work, a natural occurrence allowed by God. There's nothing in our control to stop it, except to plan for safety as best we can. But even in our best situations, some storms, like tornadoes or hurricanes, can come and take everything away. We have every right to fear their power.

In life, we face storms too. They might not always bring the full course of high winds, thunder, and lightning, but they still have the ability to wreak havoc. Storms can affect our families, our finances, our health, and our everyday lives. A storm is a situation that isn't self-inflicted, not due to a lack of stewardship or disobedience. It's when you've done all you know to do, and the storm still comes.

Maybe it's a sudden economic downturn, a natural disaster wiping out your warehouse, the rules of the game changing overnight, a new law, a new competitor, or a global pandemic. Or perhaps, it was an employee making an honest mistake that was very costly. Whatever it is, you're in it now, and the only way out is through.

In these moments, you have two choices: panic or trust the process. The storm doesn't stop because of your feelings. It's going to do what it's going to do. You have the power to adapt, lead your team through it, and be open to understanding its purpose. The storm tests your resilience, your preparation, and your faith. It's not personal—it's just life. But how do you respond? That's where your leadership shines.

Remember, you're the co-captain of your ship, and no matter what comes your way, you don't sail alone. God is with you in the storm, giving you peace when the winds and the waves are high. The challenges will come, but they don't define you. What defines you is how you respond—how you lead.

I remember those days back in Illinois like it was yesterday, grabbing our bikes and riding through the aftermath of the storm like it was some kind of adventure. To us kids, it wasn't destruction—it was a maze waiting to be explored. We didn't fear it; we were too caught up in the excitement.

But as adults, storms hit differently. We know what's on the line now. We see the risks, the damage, the potential for everything to come crashing down. That weight—the responsibility—makes the fear real. It's not just a game anymore; it's life. And because of that, we prepare, we brace ourselves, we try to control everything we can. But no matter how much we prepare, we can't control the storm itself. And that's where faith comes in—not blind faith, but a faith that lets you face the storm like a child again.

> **WHEN YOU ANCHOR YOURSELF TO THE ONE WHO BUILDS IT ALL, THE STORM DOESN'T OWN YOU.**

As kids, our faith teetered on how we were led. We trusted our parents to figure it out, to guide us through. That's the kind of faith we need now—not in people, but in the ultimate Builder of All Things. The wisdom of my adulthood says to take the storm seriously. Be prepared. But the faith of my childhood says, "You'll get through it, so trust the process." What if we approached every storm—every trial in life—with that balance? Smart enough to prepare, but brave enough to let go and trust?

It's not easy. Fear will whisper worst-case scenarios, but faith reminds us that there's something beyond the storm. You don't have to enjoy the chaos, but you can embrace the adventure of navigating through it, knowing that tomorrow is a new opportunity. And when you anchor yourself to the One who builds it all, the storm doesn't own you. You ride through it like those bike rides after the storm, knowing you're going to make it to the other side.

Those storms taught me lessons I carry to this day. As a kid, counting the seconds between lightning and thunder was our way of gauging how close the storm was. Life's challenges are no different—if we're paying attention, the signs are always there. Maybe it's a gut feeling or a shift in the atmosphere, but we often know when something's coming.

> **STORMS AREN'T PUNISHMENTS OR PROOF WE'RE OFF TRACK; THEY'RE JUST LIFE HAPPENING.**

And when it does, it's on us to prepare—secure what we can, protect what matters most, and brace ourselves. But even with all the preparation in the world, some storms hit harder than we would have ever expected. They'll shake what we thought was unshakable. It's okay to feel that weight, to cry, to acknowledge the struggle. What's not okay is giving up. Storms don't last forever. When they pass, there's always an opportunity to rebuild.

Storms aren't punishments or proof we're off track; they're just life happening. And while we can't control the storm, we can control how we respond. Faith over fear. Action over being stagnant. Hope over despair. Every leader and every person faces these moments. The measure of a leader isn't how they perform in calm waters—it's how they rise when the storm hits.

THE WINDS, LIGHTNING, THUNDER, AND RAIN OF THE STORM

I remember when Tiffany and I were building our dream, and everything felt like it was aligning with our purpose. Each year, our revenue wasn't just increasing—it was doubling. It was thrilling, like watching the vision unfold right before our eyes. We had an incredible team by our side, and the projects we'd only dared to imagine were finally coming our way. People began to trust our brand, and we were making our mark across the island of Hawai'i. People started stopping us in grocery stores, on hikes, and even at the mall, recognizing our company logo on my shirt. They'd come up and say they follow us on Instagram and love what we're doing. How cool is that?

The heavy weight I'd been carrying as a business owner started to lift. Everything was running smoothly, like a well-oiled machine, allowing me to focus on guiding the ship instead of being caught up in the daily grind. Working on the company and not necessarily in it. Our meetings were efficient, and our systems were pretty solid. We had plans in place to handle any bumps in the road—especially when it came to our finances.

Tiffany and I were meticulous about keeping an eye on our money, regularly checking reports, and making sure everything added up. But then, little warning signs started to appear. Despite all the projects and revenue pouring in, we began to notice our bank accounts didn't match what the books were showing. Something wasn't right. That's when I felt it—the wind of a storm brewing. I couldn't see it yet, but something about that wind felt different. So, I dug in.

We went through every account, checked every detail, and worked late nights to figure out what was going on. Bills kept rolling in, and we put a hard stop on any big purchases until we could sort it out. The knot in my stomach tightened as I stared at the numbers. It felt like seeing lightning in the distance—now I knew for sure a storm was on its way. Something big was off.

Then I saw it. A double entry—half a million dollars, marked as a client down payment. My stomach sank, like the thunder had just slammed its first warning. It wasn't just any month. It happened during a time when our revenue was significantly lower than normal, yet the mistake aligned almost perfectly with our monthly expectations, allowing it to slip under the radar.

For six months, we'd been operating under the illusion of a surplus that didn't even exist. This was the kind of thing I never thought could happen. We trusted our accounting firm—the experts we paid to reconcile every statement, double-check every detail, and make sure everything was spot on. We handed over everything, thinking errors like this just weren't possible. But they were. And now, six months of decisions rested on a foundation that wasn't even real.

The deeper I dug, the stronger the storm grew. It wasn't just lightning in the distance anymore. The thunder cracked overhead. The storm wasn't coming—it was already here.

An error—a single administrative mistake by our accounting firm—hit us like a hurricane. When the truth came to light, the storm wasn't just brewing—it had already arrived, and it was massive.

We didn't have the luxury to panic. We cut ties with the accounting firm immediately and regrouped. Tiffany and I leaned into fasting and prayer, seeking wisdom from the Builder of All Things like never before. We had to make tough calls—downsizing our team from fifty employees to half that size, closing physical locations, and pivoting our operations entirely. At the same time, inflation started to soar, interest rates froze the housing market, and permit delays across Hawai'i happened at a record rate, stalling construction projects island-wide. Our cash flow started to drain like water spilling from a busted pipe. We weren't just in the storm—we were in its eyewall, caught in the most destructive part. The eyewall is the heart of the storm's chaos—where the winds are the fiercest, the rain is relentless, and the pressure is crushing. It's the part that can tear everything apart if you're not ready.

In business, the eyewall is that moment when all the external pressures and challenges come at you full force. Unlike the calm eye at the center, the eyewall doesn't give you a break—it's where you're forced to face the storm head-on and prove whether your foundation can hold.

The weight was unbearable. I was running on fumes, now back to juggling too many roles and operating in survival mode. I felt like a ship without a rudder, drifting further from the vision and purpose that once guided us. The rain was here. We could feel, hear, and see its effects. The storm had stripped everything away, leaving us raw, exposed, and questioning how to move forward. But sometimes, it takes losing your footing to remember who really has control of your path.

WAKING UP THE BUILDER

It was like in Mark 4:35-41 (ESV):

> *On that day, when evening had come, he said to them, "Let us go across to the other side." And leaving the crowd, they took him with them in the boat, just as he was. And other boats were with him. And a great windstorm arose, and the waves were breaking into the boat, so that the boat was already filling. But he was in the stern, asleep on the cushion. And they woke him and said to him, "Teacher, do you not care that we are perishing?" And he awoke and rebuked the wind and said to the sea, "Peace! Be still!" And the wind ceased, and there was a great calm. He said to them, "Why are you so afraid? Have you still no faith?" And they were filled with great fear and said to one another, "Who then is this, that even the wind and the sea obey him?"*

In this story, Jesus slept in a boat during a violent storm while His disciples panicked. The winds grew, waves crashed over the sides, and fear took hold of them. They woke him in desperation, asking, "How can you sleep at a time like this?" Jesus stood, spoke directly to the storm, and instantly the chaos calmed. His disciples were left stunned, wondering, *Who is this that even the wind and waves obey him?*

There's something about a storm that reveals the truth of a situation, doesn't it? You can often tell just by looking into the eyes of your leader. Are they calm? Are they steady? Or is there fear hiding there? In moments of chaos, those eyes will tell you everything.

Imagine a ship so massive, so impressive, that the world called it unsinkable. The *Titanic*. It wasn't just a boat; it was a symbol of human achievement. But underneath all that was a weakness no one could see. A single iceberg tore through its hull and sealed its fate in just a few hours.

Maybe you've never seen the movie or heard much about the *Titanic*. That's okay. At its core, the story isn't about the ship itself. It's about what happens when people face a crisis they can't control.

There's a moment in the movie *Titanic* where Rose (played by Kate Winslet), a young woman on board, looks to Mr. Andrews, who was the architect of this massive ship. I'm sure this reflects real-life moments when people turned to him for answers when the chaos hit. She realizes something's wrong. She doesn't want comforting lies; she wants reality. She's aware that he's the only one who knows the entirety of the ship—I mean, he designed it. She looks him in the eyes and says, "Mr. Andrews, tell me the truth. What's wrong with the ship?" And he gives it to her straight: "It will sink."[18]

Now, let's consider the story of the small fishing boat, battered by massive waves and its crew overwhelmed by fear. Their leader, Jesus, isn't shouting commands or rallying the team. He's asleep. Can you imagine that? The storm is getting

---

18 James Cameron, *Titanic* (released December 19, 1997; Los Angeles, CA: Paramount Pictures).

out of control, and the One they're counting on is lying there, completely at peace. The disciples are panicking. They wake him up in desperation, probably thinking, *How can you sleep through this? Don't you care?* Like Rose sought Mr. Andrews, the architect of the boat.

But here's the thing. Jesus wasn't worried. He stood, looked at the chaos around him, and spoke three words: "Peace, be still." Instantly, the storm obeyed. Just like that. Remember, He was the one who set the GPS and said, "Let us go across to the other side."

He had control the whole time. Even when it looked like He was distant. Even when it seemed like He wasn't paying attention. That storm, as powerful as it seemed, was no match for Him.

Life will hit you with things you can't control—things that feel unstoppable. But in those moments, who are you looking to? The Architect of the Boat or the Builder of All Things? You're not alone in your storm. Whether you believe in divine power or not, there's something to be said about finding strength in someone greater who can steady you when the waves threaten to pull you under.

One morning, after the eyewall of our business storm hit—the accounting error, the layoffs, the financial strain—I hit my breaking point. Exhausted, overwhelmed, and out of answers, I finally did something I hadn't done enough: I turned my frustration into gratitude. I started thanking the Builder for every blessing we still had, even as the storm raged. I promised to stay grateful no matter what. And then, in one raw, desperate moment, I cried out, *Wake up! I can't handle this storm alone. I need rest!*

What happened next wasn't some instant miracle that wiped away all the problems. Instead, it was something deeper—a shift inside me. It was like I remembered who was on this boat with us, the One who had set the course and knew exactly where we were headed. Peace and clarity rushed in, like the sunlight breaking through after the storm. The waves were still there, and the wind was still blowing, but the storm didn't own me anymore.

That's when I realized: the Builder of All Things had been there the whole time. Every gust of wind, every flash of lightning, every crack of thunder. He'd never left. As co-captains of this ship, Tiffany and I had learned how to adjust our sails and spot the warning signs of incoming storms. But we also learned something even more important: the power of waking Jesus out of faith, not fear. Fear says, "Don't you care?" Faith says, "We trust You've got this." And let me tell you, that changes everything.

It's like having the confidence of a kid again—knowing there's someone bigger, stronger, and wiser taking care of things. You're not waking Him to save you because you're panicking; you're waking Him because you trust Him to lead you through it. Like Rose asking the architect of the *Titanic*, we had to go straight to the source, the Builder of All Things, and seek the truth.

We can't avoid every storm, but we did learn how to embrace them, knowing they were part of the journey. Storms are going to come—that's just life. But we didn't have to face them alone. With the Builder of All Things on board, we had the One who commands the seas, the wind, and the waves. And that was more than enough.

The storm wasn't the end of the story; it was just a chapter, and we trusted that He was still steering us toward the destination He had planned all along.

Looking back now, that storm—man, as terrifying as it felt in the moment—was exactly what we needed. At the time, dealing with the chaos from our accounting firm felt like it might take us under. I was pouring so much of my energy into fixing the problem that it started to take over everything. I felt like I had to be accountable for it all—for every project, every decision. And yeah, we were finishing the projects strong, but the weight of that focus came with a cost. My attention was so locked on solving the issue in front of me that I started losing sight of the bigger picture—and with it, we started losing profits.

The market was going wild—prices skyrocketing, permits dragging out longer and longer—and we were barely holding on. But here's the truth: God was on board the whole time. He had us on His stream, guiding us toward our purpose and destination, even though it didn't feel like it.

That storm forced us to face some hard realities. It wasn't just a storm for the sake of chaos—it was God's way of changing our direction. If we hadn't gone through it, we wouldn't have survived the storm that continued to happen in the housing market. Inflation kept climbing, permit delays kept stacking up, and what we thought was stability turned out to be shaky ground. But that shake-up led us to make the pivots that saved us. We scaled back, tightened up, and found a new rhythm with larger, high-end luxury projects. We didn't just survive; we found a way to thrive.

I'll never forget the team meeting I called during that time in 2022. I sat everyone down and laid it out with total transparency. I didn't sugarcoat it. I told them exactly what we were up against—the storm we were in and what it was going to take to get through it. I shared the vision, how we'd stop spreading ourselves thin across too many jobs and instead pull together as one team. We'd focus on fewer, bigger projects, and we'd survive it together.

And you know what? That shift didn't just change how we worked; it changed who we were as a team. Although we lost a lot of good employees, we came out stronger, tighter, and more focused. That kind of growth doesn't happen without the storm. The storm wasn't just a challenge. This storm was a gift, God's way of aligning us with the path we were supposed to be on all along.

THREE WAYS TO FACE THE STORM

Going through this season, I've developed some effective tactics that I'm excited to share with you. There are three ways we can face a storm, and we will look at these below. However, first, there are two different approaches we should consider.

The first is ***practical risk management***, which means having a solid system in place to recognize when a storm is coming and how to prepare for it. In this chapter, I'll walk you through three sensory indicators—ways to feel, hear, and see the risks before they fully hit. These aren't just theories;

they're practical tools you can apply directly to your business to help navigate challenges with clarity and control.

The second is ***spiritual management***—your perspective and mindset when you're already in the storm. It's about how you see the trial, how you move through it, and how you trust God to lead you through the chaos. Because let's be honest: storms are inevitable. No matter how much you prepare, some challenges will push you beyond your limits. When that happens, your spiritual posture can make all the difference between breaking under pressure or finding strength you didn't know you had.

We're going to explore both sides—practical and spiritual—because I believe the two go hand in hand. On the practical side, I'll show you how to read the wind, thunder, and lightning as indicators of risk in your business. On the spiritual side, I'll share lessons I've learned about perspective and faith when everything feels like it's falling apart.

You see, storms test us. They test our preparation, our leadership, and our ability to stay anchored. But they also have the power to refine us, to strip away what's weak, and leave us stronger. Whether you're leading a business, a team, or just trying to navigate life, understanding how to face storms practically and spiritually will prepare you to weather the storm.

By the end of this chapter, my hope is that you'll have a framework to not only survive the storm but to grow through it, both as a leader and as a person. Because storms don't just come to destroy; they come to reveal what we're really made of.

> **WHEN I STARTED LISTENING TO THOSE SMALL NUDGES, I DISCOVERED I COULD PREVENT THE STORM FROM ESCALATING.**

PRACTICAL RISK MANAGEMENT

THE WIND (FEELING THE RISK)

Navigating business storms begins with the wind—those moments when something feels off, but you can't quite put your finger on it. This is your gut telling you to slow down and pay attention. Feeling the wind comes naturally from years of experience in our craft. It's that intuition and discernment that gets built up over time, shaped by the lessons we've learned and the challenges we've faced. But let's be real—it's not just something we develop on our own. That gut feeling, that nudge we can't explain? That's God working inside of us, fine-tuning our instincts to prepare us for what's ahead. The wind is His way of saying, *Pay attention.* It's subtle, but if you're in tune with it, it can save you from a storm you didn't even see coming.

In my own business, I've learned that ignoring the wind often leads to bigger problems later. When I started listening to those small nudges, I discovered I could prevent the storm from escalating. The wind reminds us to pause, ask questions, and lean into discernment. A great business owner knows how to feel the tension in the air and act before it thickens.

THUNDER (HEARING THE RISK)

The thunder comes next, and it's louder, undeniable. You start hearing the risks from every direction—employee concerns, industry trends, or client dissatisfaction. This is when you must tune in. Risk management at this stage means sorting through the noise and identifying what really matters. I've faced times when thunder rolled loud in my ears, and the temptation was to react to every sound. But not every rumble signals lightning. As a leader, you need to stay calm, prioritize, and communicate clearly with your team. Ask the tough questions: What's the most critical threat right now? What's the worst-case scenario? Once you have clarity, start preparing for the inevitable.

LIGHTING (SEEING THE RISK)

When lightning strikes, there's no more guessing. You see the problem clearly, and it's impossible to ignore. This is where real leadership shows up. I remember a client once pulled out of a major project at the last minute, and the fallout hit hard. But, the groundwork I had laid during the wind and thunder stages gave me the tools to respond effectively. Lightning requires action—not panic. You gather your team, execute the plan, and contain the damage.

RAIN IN THE STORM

Then comes the rain. You feel it, you hear it, you see it all at once. It's the full force of the storm, and you're in the middle of it. This is where your preparation pays off. In business, the rain is often the most chaotic part—employees stressed, resources stretched, managers questioning your every move. But survival in the rain isn't about doing everything perfectly; it's about staying steady and trusting the process. Stick to your risk plan but remain flexible enough to adjust as new challenges emerge. Communicate constantly, monitor progress in real-time, and lean on your team. No one survives a storm alone.

And here's the truth about storms: they end. The rain doesn't last forever, and when the skies clear, you'll see the lessons it left behind. Every storm I've encountered has taught me something new about my business and myself. It showed me the cracks in my system, revealed the strength of my team, and reminded me of the importance of preparation. The storms will come—there's no avoiding that. But if you learn to feel the wind, hear the thunder, and act when lightning strikes, you'll not only survive; you'll emerge stronger.

SPIRITUAL MANAGEMENT

Spiritual management is about positioning our perspective to see beyond the chaos, trusting the Builder of All Things to guide us. It's not about avoiding challenges—it's about recognizing when to call on Him, leaning on His wisdom, and allowing His presence to shape our response. With the right perspective, even the fiercest storms can lead to growth.

FACING THE STORM ALONE

Imagine setting sail without consulting the Builder of All Things. You head out to your own destination. You're far from shore, battling waves with no compass and no plan. Many people go through life like this, navigating storms without hope or guidance. And yet, even when they cry out in desperation, the Builder hears them.

Sometimes, the help we need arrives in ways we don't recognize—like Jesus walking on water toward his friends. Fear blinds us to the solution, and we mistake help for something to fear:

> *Later that night, he was there alone, and the boat was already a considerable distance from land, buffeted by the waves because the wind was against it. Shortly before dawn Jesus went out to them, walking on the lake. When the disciples saw him walking on the lake, they were terrified. "It's a ghost," they said, and cried out in fear. —Matthew 14:24-26*

Trying to navigate life without seeking God's guidance is like setting sail without a compass or a plan—eventually, you'll feel overwhelmed and lost. Many of us go through challenges this way, not realizing the help we need is closer than we think. The story of Jesus walking on water reminds us that fear can blind us to God's presence and provision. Stay open and receptive to His help, even when it comes in unexpected ways.

THE BUILDER OF ALL THINGS IS ON BOARD, BUT YOU DON'T ASK FOR HELP

Now, picture being in the storm with the Builder of All Things right there in your boat, but you try to handle everything yourself. Waves crash over, the storm rages, but you keep pushing, relying only on your own strength.

> **IGNORING HIM ISN'T STRENGTH, AND ASKING FOR HELP ISN'T WEAKNESS— IT'S WISDOM IN ACTION.**

I've been there—trying to fix everything on my own, even though I knew He was with me. I thought letting him "sleep" was a sign of my faith. But the truth is, waking Him up isn't a sign of weakness; it's a sign of wisdom.

> *"Suddenly a furious storm came up on the lake, so that the waves swept over the boat. But Jesus was sleeping."*
> —Matthew 8:24

The Builder of All Things is always with us, even when we fail to lean on Him. Picture Him in the boat during the storm, yet we try to handle everything ourselves. It's a classic human tendency to rely on our own strength, but thinking we can fix it all alone doesn't show faith; it shows misplaced effort.

Faith isn't passive; it's actively seeking His help. Ignoring Him isn't strength and asking for help isn't weakness—it's wisdom in action.

WAKING HIM UP

Finally, imagine waking Him up during the storm. You cry out, "Save us! We're going to drown!"

His response might challenge you: "Why are you afraid? Where is your faith?" But then, with three words, He calms the storm: "Peace! Be Still!"

The Builder of All Things isn't offended when we wake Him. He wants us to turn to Him. Whether it's out of fear or faith, it's always relational. The key is waking Him with faith, knowing that He has the power to calm the chaos and guide us through.

The disciples went and woke him, saying, "Lord, save us! We're going to drown!"

He replied, "You of little faith, why are you so afraid?" Then he got up and rebuked the wind and waves, and it was completely calm.

—Matthew 8:25-26

It's okay to step beyond self-reliance and reach out to God in the middle of life's storms. Waking Jesus during the chaos isn't a sign of weakness—it's a move of wisdom and strength. Faith is relational, built on trust and connection. Whether it's fear or faith driving us to call out, God responds powerfully, calming the storm and strengthening the bond. When we turn to Him, we find peace and clarity, no matter how turbulent the waters may seem.

NAVIGATING THE STORMS TOGETHER

Storms are part of life. We can't always control when or how they come, but we can control how we respond. The choice is ours: face them alone, struggle while help is within reach, or wake the Builder of All Things and trust Him to carry us through.

Whether you're a believer or not, there's a practical truth here. Recognizing your limitations, asking for help, and trusting in a solution greater than yourself can change everything when the storm rages.

So, when you're in the thick of it, remember this: storms don't last forever. The Builder of All Things is ready—ready to calm the seas, guide your ship, and help you find your way back to peace. It's up to you to decide if you'll try to brave it alone or have the courage to wake Him and trust the process.

> **SONG PAIRING:** "Drown" by Lecrae
> feat. John Legend
> *Restoration* (Album)[19]

---

[19] Lecrae, vocalist, "Drowning," by Alex Stacey, Daniel Majic, et al., released July 17, 2020, track 7 on *Restoration*, Reach Records.

CHAPTER 7

THE SNAKE:
Air Jordan on 'Em

Taking It to the Sky

*"Does the hawk take flight by your wisdom...?
Does the eagle soar at your command...?
It dwells on a cliff.... From there it looks for food."*
—Job 39:26-29

WE CAN ELEVATE

You're a business owner grinding it out in a tough market with tough clients and tough competition. Some challenges are just part of the game. They're like the storms we talked about before. You ride them out, adjust your sails, and keep moving. But every so often, something different creeps in. It's not the usual ups and downs or just another rough day. No, this one feels personal. Like someone—or something—is intentionally trying to take you down. This isn't business as usual; it's betrayal, sabotage, or deceit. It's a snake in the grass, and its bite cuts deep.

When this happens, you can feel the venom. You start second-guessing yourself, wondering what you did to deserve it. Maybe you feel blindsided, powerless, or just plain frustrated. The good news is there's a way through this. You can't handle the snake by wrestling in the dirt. You've got to do something different. You have to rise above the battleground and the enemy's tactics. You need to elevate.

There's no standard business manual for dealing with snakes. Most advice out there tells you how to handle normal conflicts or challenging market conditions, but what do you do when you feel personally attacked? How do you respond when it's not just a storm, but a snake twisting itself around your ankles to trip you? Maybe even your neck to suffocate you?

For me, the key to dealing with this came from an unlikely place: it was inspired by my childhood love of basketball. I didn't realize it at the time, but watching the game as a kid planted seeds of wisdom I'd use years later in the business world. You might think playing sports and business are different universes, but let me tell you, the principles overlap more than you'd expect. On the basketball court, you learn how to handle defenders who want nothing more than to shut you down. You learn to spot opportunities, seize the moment, and rise above the opposition. That same mindset can help you stand strong against the snakes in business.

WHY BASKETBALL?

Basketball was a big part of my upbringing. My family has deep roots in the sport. My grandpa, Don Mathews, helped Bradley University become NCAA Division One runner-up champions in 1954. Later, my uncle Eddie Mathews won an NIT championship with Bradley in 1982. Both men went on to become successful high school coaches and eventually earned their places in the Illinois Basketball Hall of Fame. They didn't just love basketball—they lived it. Growing up, basketball games, coaching sessions, and endless talk about strategy were woven into the fabric of my life.

I remember when I was about ten years old, my dad brought home our first basketball hoop. We climbed onto the garage roof to set it up, just him and me. Afterward, we played game after game—one-on-one, HORSE, you name it. He never went easy on me. He promised that one day I'd beat him, and when that day came, it'd be his last time playing me. Until then, he'd keep pushing, keep challenging, and keep reminding me that growth doesn't happen when things are easy. It happens when you face adversity head-on.

That kind of raw, honest competition taught me something big at a young age: you don't run from tough situations. You face them. You adapt. You learn to read the defense. In basketball, when the other team plays man-to-man, focusing on you, sticking to you like glue, what do you do? You look for the gap, the chance to drive to the rim. You know if you make your move at the right time, you can rise above their defense and score.

The same principle applies in business. When the snake zeroes in on you, trying to steal your confidence, reputation, or peace of mind, you can't just roll over. You've got to find that opening, that moment to elevate above the rim.

AIR JORDAN AND THE ART OF ELEVATION

I grew up in the nineties, watching Michael Jordan. Let's be honest: who didn't watch him? My dad was a die-hard Bulls fan during the MJ era. We watched every game we could. Jordan changed the way we saw basketball—he wasn't just another player; he was the standard. His nickname, "Air Jordan," spoke volumes. While other players jumped, Jordan soared. He didn't just leap; he seemed to hang in the air indefinitely, defying gravity, gliding past defenders who were already on their way back down.

There's an old Coca-Cola commercial that's stuck in my mind. Three kids are in a treehouse and forget to bring up the drinks. So, they call out, "Michael!" Suddenly, Michael Jordan appears, leaping up to the treehouse window, handing them a six-pack of soda while hanging in the air, as if it were the easiest thing in the world. He just hung there, mid-air, smiling. It sounds silly, but we all semi-believed he could do that. It captured something real: Jordan could kind of "fly," and everyone knew it.

Jordan's ability to rise above the rim wasn't just about physical talent. It represented a mindset—an approach to challenges. While defenders tried to stop him using standard tactics, Jordan operated on another level. When they jumped, he lingered. When they reached, he hung longer. He finished the play while in the air as they were already descending. Watching him showed me that true victory often comes from going higher than the opposition expects you to.

When I was older, I stumbled across a hip-hop track by K-Drama called "Air Jordan." The lyrics of the chorus are, "Opposition in my face, trying to play defense. . . . I'm bigger than this dude, this doesn't make no sense, I Air Jordan on 'em." Those lyrics paint a vivid picture. When life throws an opponent at you—something or someone standing in your way—sometimes you just have to elevate above them. They jump; you rise higher.

This image stuck with me because it applied to more than just sports. In business and in life, the best move when faced with a relentless enemy isn't always to fight on their level. It's to rise above, to find that faith-fueled confidence that lets you play the game from a higher vantage point. In other words, you learn to soar where the enemy can't even compete.

FAITH, FLIGHT, AND THE SNAKE

As I matured, I began to see connections between basketball and faith. Just like Jordan rose above defenders, faith calls us to rise above fear, doubt, and the attacks of the enemy. The Bible often uses the image of soaring—like an eagle—as a sign of faith and trust in God. Eagles build their nests high on cliffs, surveying everything from a vantage point that leaves predators down below.

In business, you run into plenty of predators. Some are just tough breaks or challenging competitors. But others have a personal edge to them. They feel like snakes: sneaky, crafty, working behind the scenes to twist facts or undermine your efforts. The snake might show up as a partner who betrays confidential information, a competitor who spreads false rumors, or a client who blackmails you with lies posted online. When faced with these attacks, many of us either fight back with emotion or run away in despair. But there's another option: flight in the spiritual sense doesn't mean retreating. It means elevating. It means lifting the battle to a place where the snake can't fight.

DON'T FIGHT THE SNAKE ON ITS TERMS.

An eagle never wrestles with a snake on the ground. Why? Because that's the snake's strength. On the ground, the snake can wrap around you, strike, and use its venom. But the eagle is smarter. It swoops down, grabs the snake, and takes off. In the air, the snake is helpless—it can't wrap around the eagle, strike, or fight back. Once the eagle reaches a high altitude, it lets go, and the snake falls to its defeat.

The lesson is simple: don't fight the snake on its terms. In business and life, the "snake" can be anything—betrayal, lies, or personal attacks. Snakes thrive in low places like fear, anger, and chaos. If you stay there, wrestling with them emotionally or reacting out of panic, you're giving them the upper hand. But like the eagle, you're not built for the ground. You're made to rise and elevate the problem. Eagles don't wrestle in the mud. They soar above, let go, and let gravity do the rest. Take the battle to the sky and leave the snake behind. That's how you win.

A good friend of mine, a doctor, once explained to me about the fight-or-flight response to stress. It's our body's built-in alarm system that kicks in when we feel threatened. In a business scenario, "fight" often means pushing harder, refusing to back down, and meeting force with force. "Flight" might mean backing off, quitting, or avoiding the problem altogether. But I've learned that spiritually, flight means something else. Instead of running away, you go higher. You give the problem over to God. You trust that He sees what you can't. You let Him guide your strategy, and suddenly, you're operating from a vantage point the snake cannot reach.

Think of it like choosing to hang in the air a little longer, just like Jordan. You're not ignoring the problem. You're just not letting it suck you into the mud. You're taking it to the sky.

MY ENCOUNTER WITH A SNAKE

I remember facing my first real snake in business. We had a small contract through a big box store, just a few thousand dollars and a handful of days' work. Compared to our larger projects, this seemed easy. On the second day, the client complained about an installation issue. That happens in construction. Usually, you apologize, fix it, and move on. But this client refused to let us back on the property to correct the mistake. Instead, he demanded money. We followed protocol and alerted the big box store. Typically, they'd mediate, supervise a solution, or bring in another contractor. But this client wouldn't cooperate. He escalated his demands, sending out email blasts, flooding social media with false accusations, and even personally attacking my wife with verbal abuse through email. He started using PayPal links to demand payments, blackmailing us, threatening our reputation, and spending thousands on ads to smear our name online.

This wasn't a tough client anymore. This was a personal attack. The stress felt crushing. Reviews are the lifeblood of a construction business, and this guy was on a mission to destroy our image. I tried fighting back at first, defending myself in every arena, by calling lawyers and figuring out my options. But the stress was suffocating. Eventually, I wanted to run, to escape it all.

Then it hit me: this was a snake. It wasn't about the money or the job. It was about tearing down what we'd built. The enemy was using this situation to poke at my fears, insecurities, and sense of purpose. Recognizing the snake changed how I responded. It reminded me that I needed a different strategy—one that involved elevating the fight to flight.

DISCERNING THE SNAKE

Not every problem in your business is a snake. Some are just storms—tough seasons you have to weather. A snake, on the other hand, is intentional. It aims to knock you off your path. It strikes where you're vulnerable and tries to derail you from your purpose. Snakes thrive on confusion, fear, and emotional reactions. They're not just random troubles; they're personal attacks on your mindset and mission. Knowing the difference matters. If you treat a snake like a storm, you might try to endure it when you should be outsmarting it. If you treat a storm like a snake, you'll waste energy fighting something that just needs time and steady handling. Discernment is key.

I realized what we were dealing with—it was a snake. Not the person, but the enemy working through the situation, trying to get to us. This wasn't a storm; it was something different. The snake's tactics aren't complicated; in fact, they're pretty predictable.

Let's break it down and expose it. The snake operates with the same playbook every time—bait, hook, and kill. It's like fishing. First, it patiently lures you in with bait, waiting for you to bite. Once you're hooked, it reels you in, trying to gain control. And finally, it goes for the kill, aiming to take you out completely. That's exactly what was happening here. This client wasn't just challenging our work; the attacks were personal. The emails were aimed at my beliefs, the verbal jabs brought fear and stress, and the public posts were designed to tarnish everything we'd built. The snake was working overtime.

THE BAIT

The enemy wants to steal your perspective. Yes, that's right—your perspective! The idea of a "snake" comes straight out of the Bible's first pages, described as a sneaky, cunning force that twists how you see things. Picture something working in the background, subtly planting doubts or distractions. This snake wants to hijack your view—how you define what's important and valuable.

Your perspective is what shapes your decisions, your company culture, and the legacy you're building. But here's the hard truth: the moment you commit to running your business with purpose and higher standards, you're going to attract attention, the wrong kind. Adversity will start creeping in, crafted to throw you off course, distract you, and keep you from flowing forward in the stream of purpose you've worked so hard to navigate.

Let's talk about staying sharp because in business—and life—you've got to keep your head in the game. First Peter 5:8 portrays it like this: "Be *alert* and of sober mind. Your enemy the devil prowls around like a roaring lion looking for someone to devour."

Think about it, challenges don't just happen randomly. Sometimes, they feel like they're coming straight for you, calculated and relentless. It's like facing an opponent who knows your weaknesses and is ready to exploit them.

Now, let's dive into why the idea of a "snake" is such a big deal in the Bible. Two key stories highlight this image. First, the story of the snake in Genesis, which reveals how the enemy works. Adam and Eve were the first humans, living in this perfect place called the Garden of Eden. Everything they needed was right there. They were given one rule: don't eat the fruit from a specific tree—the tree of the knowledge of good and evil. Simple, right? But then, the snake shows up.

Second, the story of Jesus being tempted in the wilderness shows the same tactics in action. Jesus has just been baptized, and He's gearing up for His mission. But before He gets started, He heads out into the wilderness for forty days. No food. No comforts. Just Him, His thoughts, and meditation time. This sounds like a task I don't think I could ever accomplish on my own. But here's where it gets even crazier: during this time, the snake shows up.

Now, here's the thing: **the snake shows up right there** in the thick of it. It's almost like the snake was watching and thought, *If I'm gonna strike, I've got to hit Him now. He's hungry, He's isolated, He's vulnerable.* And isn't that relatable? It's often in our wilderness moments—when we're worn out, questioning, and barely hanging on—that the temptations, doubts, and lies slither their way into our minds.

> **THE SNAKE'S GAME MIGHT BE CRAFTY, BUT ONCE YOU IDENTIFY IT FOR WHAT IT IS, YOU'VE ALREADY GOT THE UPPER HAND.**

The stories of Adam and Eve in the garden and Jesus in the wilderness show us something big: the tactics of the snake—the enemy—are consistent. Whether it's twisting truths, appealing to desires, or planting doubt, the approach hasn't changed since day one.

Why a snake (serpent)? Well, Genesis 3:1 describes it like this: "Now the serpent was more crafty than any of the wild animals the LORD God had made." Crafty, sneaky, manipulative—that's the snake's M.O. In this story. The snake questions

Eve with a seemingly innocent line: "Did God really say, 'You must not eat *from* any tree in the garden?'"

This is classic bait-and-switch. The snake plants a seed of doubt, questioning what's true and getting you to second-guess yourself. It's the same move in business or leadership—someone challenges your decisions, your values, or even your worth, just enough to throw you off balance.

Fast forward to Jesus in the wilderness. Here's what happens: "The *tempter* came to him and said, 'If you are the Son of God, tell these stones to become bread'" (Matthew 4:3).

The snake's tactic here is to provoke Jesus to prove Himself. It's like saying, "You think you're the real deal? Prove it!" But Jesus doesn't take the bait. The snake works hard to blind or distort your perspective. When you're stepping into your purpose—building a business, leading a team, or simply chasing a goal—the enemy doesn't just attack your actions; they go after your mindset. The bait might come as subtle doubts, whispers of self-reliance, or direct attacks on your belief system. So, how do you spot the bait?

Ask yourself:

1) Is this challenging the truth with lies?
2) Is this pushing me toward unhealthy self-reliance?
3) Is this undermining my core beliefs or values?

When you recognize these moves for what they are, you'll be better equipped to face them head-on without falling for the trap. The snake's game might be crafty, but once you identify it for what it is, you've already got the upper hand.

THE HOOK

Let's dive into what I call "the hook." This is when the enemy doesn't just mess with your mind or beliefs—he goes straight for your physical body and your emotions. Think of it like fishing. The bait looks tempting, right? It's shiny, appealing, and feels like it's meant just for you. But once you bite, the hook sets. And now? You're no longer in control. You're being dragged across the water, fighting against something stronger than you ever expected.

This "hook" attacks your flesh, your physical and emotional self. It could be addiction, stress, sickness, or even emotional reaction and pain. It's designed to take hold and wear you down. Let me show you how this plays out in those two key stories from the Bible. First, back in Genesis, the snake whispers to Eve as she stands in front of the forbidden fruit. He says, "You will not certainly die" (Genesis 3:4).

Think about that for a second. The snake is lying straight to her face, downplaying the consequences. He's saying, "It's fine. You'll be okay. Go ahead." But the truth? He knows it's a lie. He knows this choice leads to harm, but he makes it look harmless—attractive even. Eve bites the bait, and the rest is history.

Now let's jump forward to Jesus's story. When Jesus is fasting in the wilderness for forty days, the enemy shows up and tries to hook Him:

"If you are the Son of God," he said, "throw yourself down. For it is written: 'He will command his angels concerning you, and they will lift you up in their

> *hands, so that you will not strike your foot against a stone.'" —Matthew 4:6*

The snake is daring Jesus to test God—to put His identity and trust on the line. It's like saying, "Prove it! Let's see if you're really who you say you are." But Jesus doesn't bite. He knows the game. He sees the hook behind the bait and refuses to fall for it. Literally.

> **THE SNAKE WANTS TO FLIP YOUR ROLE FROM STEWARD— SOMEONE MANAGING AND BUILDING WITH PURPOSE— TO THINKING YOU'RE THE OWNER OF IT ALL.**

Now, what does this mean for you as a business owner? The hook shows up in ways that feel personal—whether it's stress that keeps you up at night, a bad habit you're justifying, or even self-doubt that makes you question your path. It grabs hold of your vulnerabilities and uses them to pull you off course.

Here's how you can spot the hook before it sets:

1) Are you justifying things that harm you?
2) Whether it's an addiction, unchecked stress, or ignoring health issues, are you convincing yourself it's "not that bad"?

3) Are your weaknesses being exploited?
4) Is there something about your situation or emotions that's making you more vulnerable right now? Recognize those areas so you can protect them.
5) Are you questioning your purpose or worth?
6) Has your confidence been shaken? Are you starting to believe lies about who you are or what you're capable of?

The key is to recognize when the hook is trying to dig in. The sooner you see it, the easier it is to wiggle free. Don't let the enemy drag you across the water. Stay grounded, keep your perspective clear, and don't bite the bait. It's never worth it.

THE KILL

The snake's ultimate move is to dismantle your belief system and pull you away from your purpose. He'll do whatever it takes to make you think you're on your own—convincing you that you don't need anyone else—not even the Builder of All Things to run your business or life. That's how he sets you up for the crash—taking down your values, your purpose, and everything you've worked for. In the garden, the snake whispered to Eve: "You will be like God" (Genesis 3:5).

He wasn't just offering her a snack; he was trying to shift her mindset. The snake's goal was to make her believe she didn't need to rely on anyone else. She could take control, be her own boss, and call the shots. But that's a trap. The snake wants to flip your role from steward—someone managing and building with purpose—to thinking you're the owner of it all. Once he's got you there, it's easy for him to sink your ship.

In the wilderness, the same snake tried to pull the same stunt with Jesus. He showed Jesus all the kingdoms of the world and said, "All this I will give you... if you will bow down and worship me" (Matthew 4:8-9).

The snake tried to distract Jesus with the illusion of control, power, and instant success, hoping to pull Him off His mission. But Jesus didn't fall for it. Here's the thing: the snake is always going for the kill. He wants to blind you with a lie and convince you to chase after every shiny opportunity and distraction instead of staying aligned with your purpose. It's his classic move, showing you what you *could* have if you just step out of the stream and try to conquer the ocean on your own.

If the snake can keep you distracted and disconnected, he's got the upper hand. But Jesus puts it straight: "The thief comes only to steal and *kill* and destroy; I have come that they may have life, and have it to the full" (John 10:10).

The snake's agenda is destruction. When you recognize the snake's tactics, whether it's in the garden, the wilderness, or your own business—you can outsmart him. There is a move in the playbook that cuts off the snake's head. To help you stay clear on your purpose, resist the bait, and keep your boat in the stream where it belongs.

ATTACKING THE SNAKE

It's like switching from defensively blocking hits to throwing your own offensive attack. Here's the change of perspective: in most battles, "flight" means retreat. But in spiritual battles, "flight" means elevation. You don't wrestle the snake on the ground; you take the fight higher. Instead of trying to tackle your challenges head-on with your own strength, you lift the battle to a level where the enemy can't compete.

In 2 Chronicles 20, there is a story of a leader named Jehoshaphat, a king from way back in biblical times. At this specific time, he found himself in a tight spot. A massive army was heading his way, and he knew his forces didn't stand a chance. Now, if you're like me, your first instinct would be to gear up, call for backup, and get ready to throw down. But Jehoshaphat? He did something completely different.

Instead of focusing on the size of the problem, he turned to God. He called his people together, and they didn't strategize; they praised. Then he put singers on the front lines. Yeah, not soldiers. Singers. They marched into battle with songs of gratitude and praise, thanking God for what He'd already done and trusting Him for what was about to happen.

And check this out: the enemy lost their minds. They became so confused they started fighting each other, wiping themselves out. Jehoshaphat's army barely had to lift a finger. The battle was over before it started because they took the fight to flight, to a level where the enemy couldn't win.

That story hit home for me when I was dealing with that client who was attacking just like a straight-up snake. He was relentless—spreading lies, trying to destroy our reputation, and throwing everything he had at me. I wanted to fight fire with fire, to hit back harder and faster. Looking back, all I knew to do was what Jehoshaphat did.

I stepped back, got in my office by myself, and spoke everything I was thankful for out loud. The breath in my lungs. The times God saved me—from the fire, from war, from myself. The blessings of my wife, my kids, and their incredible spouses. My grandkids. A business that was still standing. A team that was with me in the trenches. My health, my faith, my victories.

Then, the craziest thing happened. I got an email from the big box store we were working with. Attached was a screenshot of the sabotage campaign the client had funded. Thousands of dollars were spent on ads targeting a tiny village in the Philippines. I don't even think he understood how ad marketing works or how to aim for the right audience. Over 300,000 views and clicks, all wasted. It was like watching this snake's plan collapse under its own weight. I couldn't help but laugh because it reminded me of Jehoshaphat. The enemy's best efforts turned into nothing but confusion and failure. The big box store we were working with finally issued a cease and desist letter, and everything completely stopped. Haven't heard a word since.

The snake's head is already crushed. Your job isn't to take it on alone; it's to trust Him, lift your battles through gratitude to the Builder of All Things, and watch the snake lose its bite. You don't fight in the mud where the snake is strongest. You grab the fight, take it higher, and let gratitude and praise do the heavy lifting.

When Jehoshaphat sent those singers out, it wasn't just about music. It was about declaring trust and taking the battle to higher ground. And when I chose gratitude and praise instead of anger and fear, the same thing happened. The snake lost its grip, the chaos faded, and the victory was already in motion.

GRATITUDE: THE WEAPON FOR BATTLE

Here is the thing: the Builder of All Things has the spiritual battle handled. He sees what's coming, defends you in ways you don't even realize, and promises that the enemy's attacks won't take you out. That's His job. But here, in the everyday grind, there's a weapon He's handed you for the physical and emotional fight—gratitude.

Gratitude isn't just some feel-good idea; it's practical. Logical. It helps you take control of what the enemy wants to wreck first—your emotions. Think about it: when things go sideways, what's the first thing that happens? Fear, frustration, or anger bubbles up, clouding your decisions and throwing you off balance. Gratitude flips that script. It shifts your focus from what's wrong to what's still right.

This isn't about pretending the problem doesn't exist. It's about taking a step back and saying, "Yeah, this attack is tough but look at what I still have. Look at what's working. Look at the blessings I've already been given." Gratitude clears your mind. It helps you stop reacting and start responding with clarity and purpose. It has the power to renew your perspective.

That's the real power of gratitude: it's an offensive move. Instead of letting the enemy drag you into the mud, it gives you control. Your emotions settle, your perspective sharpens, and suddenly, you're making decisions with a steady hand instead of a panicked heart.

If you ever feel like the walls are closing in, take a moment. Pause. Start making a list of what you're thankful for. Write it down, and then say it out loud. That's praise. Praise is taking that list and those thoughts and speaking them out loud to the

Builder of All Things. That's how gratitude lifts you to higher ground. The Builder of All Things has the big battle covered. Gratitude and praise are how you win in the moment. That's how Jehoshaphat knew to win when he was outnumbered. That's how you rise above and take the fight to flight—where the enemy can't follow. And if he does, he's powerless.

So, next time the enemy shows up, don't wrestle on the ground. Air Jordan on 'em. That's how you win.

> **SONG PAIRING:** "Set Me Free" by Lecrae feat. YK Osiris
> *Restoration* (Album)[20]

---

[20] Lecrae, vocalist, "Set Me Free," by Warryn Campbell, Trecina Campbell, et al., released March 20, 2020, track 2 on *Restoration*, Reach Records.

CHAPTER 8

THE SMOKE:
Self-Inflicted Wounds

Where There's Smoke, There's Fire

> *"Whoever digs a pit will fall into it."*
> —Proverbs 26:27

WHAT IS "THE SMOKE"?

One of the best things about being an entrepreneur is freedom. Freedom to chase your vision, call the shots, and build something that's yours. It's a gift, really. But here's the thing: not all **decisions** weigh the same. Some are small, no big deal. Others ripple out and impact everything. And then some challenge you. Sometimes, they come from missteps based on what you knew at the time. But with some diligence and humility, you can get back on track and back in the main flow.

Then, there are the big ones. The ones that don't just nudge you off course—they take you into a whole different stream. A stream that wasn't designed by the Builder of All Things. And that stream is rough. It can sink your business, strain your family, and pull you under if you're not careful.

As entrepreneurs, we're proud of being risk-takers, brand-builders, and opportunity-creators. We hustle hard, pouring our energy into budgets, strategies, and timelines, ensuring every little detail is dialed in. But let me ask you this: When was your last check-in with yourself? When did you actually get clear on what's going on inside?

This chapter is about something I call "the smoke." And no, I'm not talking about the kind that drifts over from your neighbor's barbecue. This smoke is different. It's sneaky. It rises up from the inside, messing with your head, clouding your vision, and chipping away at everything you've been working so hard to build. It's like a fog that makes you second-guess yourself, and if you're not careful, it can steer your life—and your business—straight into the muddy bottom of the riverbed.

Picture this: you're driving at night, and suddenly, your windshield starts to fog up. At first, you can kind of see where you're going. But as the mist thickens, you're gripping the wheel tighter, squinting to make out the road, hoping you don't miss a turn. That's what the smoke does. It creeps in and blocks your view. It keeps you from seeing what's right in front of you and what's ahead. It's not your competitors. It's not a tough market or unfair circumstances. This one's on us. It's self-inflicted.

It sneaks in through unresolved emotions, ego-driven decisions, and misaligned effort or energy—those little compromises you let slide that start to stack up. It's like a moral and mental fog, and if you don't face it head-on, it'll quietly sabotage everything you're working so hard to build. The good news is that you don't have to stay in the fog. You can clear the windshield and start seeing the road again.

Clearing the smoke isn't just about feeling better—it's about positioning yourself to run a smarter, stronger business and better serve others. When emotions like pride or resentment go unchecked, they can cloud your decisions. Maybe it's hiring the wrong person for the wrong reasons, handling feedback poorly, or taking a risky deal to prove a point. When you address the smoke, you can make choices based on facts, values, and long-term goals—not emotional reactions. It also strengthens your team. Unresolved conflicts or refusing to own up to mistakes can erode trust, but when you clear the air, you foster open communication, collaboration, and a culture of growth.

The smoke can blur the mission that started it all, tempting you to chase trends or shortcuts that don't align with your purpose. Addressing it keeps your focus sharp and your business grounded in what truly matters. A clear-headed leader can steer the ship with confidence, even when the waters get rough. It reminds me of this powerful visual: "He opened the shaft of the bottomless pit, and from the shaft rose smoke like the smoke of a great furnace, and the sun and the air were darkened with the smoke from the shaft" (Revelation 9:2, ESV).

This paints a vivid picture of what happens when smoke rises and blocks out the light. I believe certain choices we make can do the same thing—open the shaft that releases smoke into our lives, clouding our vision and darkening our path.

There was a game my grandkids used to play when they were little. They'd throw a blanket over their heads and think they were invisible. They truly believed that as long as they couldn't see us, we couldn't see them either. My grandson Liam took it even further—he'd close his eyes and convince himself he'd disappeared into the dark. One time, he kept his eyes shut for so long that he started crying, thinking he'd never be able to see again. He was terrified that he'd lost us. We had to gently open his eyelids for him, and just like that, his world was clear again.

Like my grandkids in their hide-and-seek game, pulling a blanket over their heads and thinking they're invisible, the way the smoke becomes a covering is similar. It blinds us to what's ahead and, sometimes, even to ourselves.

It makes me think about how we handle the smoke in our lives and businesses. Too often, we shut our eyes to it, pretending it's not there, hoping no one else notices either. But the longer we ignore it, the more it feels like this foggy mess is just how things are now—like we're stuck for good. Jesus hit this right on the nose when He said, "If then the light within you is darkness, how great is that darkness!" (Matthew 6:23)

It's a wake-up call. If we convince ourselves we're on the right path when we're not, we're not just off track—we're in real trouble. Because if you don't see it, you can't fix it. The truth is that there are ways to identify the smoke, clear the air, and proactively keep it clear. This is about that moment—when you realize the smoke is clouding your path, and it's time to face it, clear it, and get back to the stream that's destined for your life and business. It's not easy, but it's necessary.

THE SMOKE SCREEN

Like that thick layer of fog that blocks your view completely, it doesn't always stop there. The layers pile up until we're fully smoke-screened. We start believing lies because we can't see the truth anymore. We're stuck in this haze, vulnerable to attacks we can't even recognize.

If you're not familiar with the term, a smoke screen is a classic military tactic. In battle, smoke is used to obscure the enemy's sight—making it hard for them to see or target effectively. It sounds smart, but it's risky. It can backfire. Take World War II, for example. During the Battle of Normandy, smoke screens were used to hide Allied forces from German defenders. But in one operation, the wind shifted unexpectedly, and instead of providing cover, the smoke outlined the advancing British tanks. It gave the enemy a clear target, leading to devastating losses.

That's what smoke does in life too. It blinds you, covers your line of sight, and makes you vulnerable. And here's the danger—it doesn't just shield you from the light; it makes you a sitting duck for attacks. The enemy doesn't even need precision. When you're blind in the smoke, you're wide open to anything.

Whether it's bad decisions, distractions, or unchecked desires, the smoke in our lives can lead us off course, just like those tanks. It hides the truth, makes us susceptible, and ultimately puts us in a dangerous place. Recognizing the smoke for what it is—and clearing it before it takes over—is critical to staying on the path and out of harm's way.

FACING THE MIRROR

Writing this chapter wasn't easy. Honestly, I think reading it might be just as hard for you. It's simple to spot someone else's flaws, right? But looking in the mirror and confronting your own? That's a whole different story. I sat with it, wrestled with it, and honestly thought about skipping it altogether. But every time I tried to leave it out, I felt a nudge, like He was saying, *Don't hide this—it needs to be shared.* And let me tell you; that push wasn't comfortable, but it was necessary.

> **VULNERABILITY ISN'T JUST UNCOMFORTABLE; IT'S REFINING.**

This chapter is like a mirror. The one that makes you stop and really take a look at yourself—not the filtered version, but the raw, unedited truth. That's hard. It's heavy. But leaving it out would've meant leaving out the very heart of this book. Without this, it wouldn't hold the weight it's supposed to carry, the anchor it's meant to be for you to set sail into your purpose.

Here's the thing—vulnerability isn't just uncomfortable; it's refining. It burns away the surface-level stuff and gets down to the core. As I wrote this, it hit me: the same battles I've faced in my life—the struggles to get honest to self-correct—are the same ones many entrepreneurs and leaders face. It's universal. We all deal with it in one way or another.

The biggest challenge for business owners and entrepreneurs—and honestly, for leaders, pastors, coaches, and even parents—is this constant pressure to sell yourself. If anyone sees a crack in your armor, you feel like you'll lose value. Your product, coaching, and leadership all feel tied to this image of having it all together. So, what do we do? We put on a front. We act like everything's fine, like we've got it all under control. But let's be honest—we know that's not the truth.

Some days it's just difficult. The weight of it all can feel overwhelming. And yet, the one thing we need most—a safe space to be honest and vulnerable—is often the very thing we avoid. But vulnerability isn't weakness; it's growth. It's the key to getting better, to actually becoming the leader, the entrepreneur, or the coach you're striving to be. It's hard, no doubt, but it's necessary.

So, yeah, this chapter was difficult to write. But if it sparks something in you to face your own challenges, then it's worth it.

After twelve years in business and building relationships with so many incredible people, I've seen and heard it all—the highs, the lows, and everything in between. I've watched amazing entrepreneurs, people with so much purpose and potential, drift off course. I've seen businesses crumble, families fall apart, and good people left facing humiliation they never saw coming. It's heartbreaking, and it's real.

That's why staying focused on the mission—your mission—is absolutely critical. This isn't just some side note; it's one of the biggest trials we face, and it's one we don't talk about enough. But we need to. Because shining a light on it is how we stay grounded and move forward without losing what matters most.

In business, it's easy to be pulled in a hundred directions. Success, recognition, money—these things can be so enticing. And while we could chalk up the challenges we face to outside forces like the enemy working against us, the truth is, sometimes it's just our own desires and choices leading us off track. That's when the smoke rolls in. It clouds our vision, blinding us to the path we're meant to follow.

I get it. As entrepreneurs, the pressure is real. There's always another goal to hit, more money to make, more recognition to chase. But when we let those desires take center stage—whether it's greed, materialism, or even something as subtle as wanting to prove ourselves—we risk losing sight of what truly matters. That smoke, more often than not, is self-inflicted. The choices we make and the compromises we allow can create wounds that cut deep.

But those wounds are also preventable. Speaking from experience, I've learned this the hard way.

I've been there—grinding hard, pouring everything into the wrong things. Chasing a specific project and client that didn't align with my values, burning through resources, and having moments of neglecting the rest of the business. I got caught in times of chasing recognition, convincing myself it'd help the next deal, ignoring advice, and letting pride take over. I started overpromising without the means to deliver.

I've been in a place where my ego clouded what the business really needed at times, leading me to risky decisions and straining relationships. I've had days where I was so busy competing with others that I lost sight of sustainable growth. I let resentment build up over certain types of criticism, blaming others instead of taking ownership. This smoke clouded my judgment, cost me opportunities, and made me miss out on valuable partnerships I should've fought to protect. It's always a hard lesson.

Surviving two house fires early in my life taught me that material things can disappear in an instant. It shifted my perspective and made it easier to let go of the world's pull. But even with that perspective, I'm not immune to the struggles of my own flesh. None of us are.

So why do we get so caught up? Is it just human nature—a kind of condition in us all? If so, what's the remedy? How do we clear the smoke? The distractions and temptations are loud, no doubt. But I've found that clarity begins when we can identify specific indicators that started the fire in the first place.

The smoke might be thick, but it's not permanent. There's always a way to clear it, to find the path again. It starts with **Honesty** and **Humility,** and then comes the **Healing.** That clarity can bring us back, aligning our steps with a purpose that won't fade.

MY STORY: TWO HOUSEFIRES, ONE MESSAGE

That summer after eighth grade, we packed up the family car and headed west from Illinois to Utah to visit my dad's side of the family for a reunion. He had planned the trip for months, and we were all looking forward to it: my mom, brothers Matt and Sean, and my little sister, Catie. For me, it felt like a transition. High school was just around the corner, and this trip seemed like one of those markers in life—the kind that divides one chapter from the next. It was my first real family vacation.

The moment we arrived in Utah and pulled into the driveway, the phone was already ringing. Uncle John handed the phone to Mom, and Grandma was on the other end. She was calling with news—news that profoundly impacted and altered many paths in our lives. I stood there watching as my mom listened, and I could see it all over her face. You just know when something is wrong.

Her voice shook as she told us the news: our home, our house back in Illinois, had caught fire, and we'd lost everything. Two neighborhood kids, just eight years old, had been playing on our porch. They found an old mattress we'd left there and a gas can Dad had stored after mowing the lawn. Maybe they were just curious, messing around with matches or a lighter. Whatever it was, that spark set the mattress on fire. This scared the kids, and they ran home, spooked by what might happen. The flames hit the gas can, and the explosion that followed consumed the porch and spread through the house. Thankfully, we weren't home, and no one got hurt.

I watched as my mom and dad hugged and cried. They shared the news with us immediately. I couldn't comprehend it all at first. But we decided as a family to remain with our relatives for the planned reunion as we were homeless, and Dad needed time to figure it all out. This stay in Utah bought us some time.

Once we packed up and headed home, the drive back felt so much heavier than the drive out. My mind kept replaying everything we'd left behind—the time spent with my brothers in each room, the corner in the living room where the Christmas tree always stood, my bedroom stacked with comic books, sports cards, and all the memories I'd built there. I tried to brace myself for what we'd find, but nothing could've prepared me.

When we pulled into the neighborhood, the smell of smoke hit us first. It hung in the air like a sour memory, sharp and bitter. As we walked up the driveway, the soot smell grew. From the street, we could see the damage. The front porch, where it all started, was a blackened skeleton of charred beams. The windows were shattered, and the walls were streaked with dark trails of soot.

The fire chief met us at the door and walked us through what was left. Inside, it was total destruction. The fire had ripped through the furniture and walls, but it was the smoke that had done the most damage. It seeped into everything—the walls, floors, ceilings—nothing was spared. The chief pointed out the burn patterns, showing where the flames had burned the hottest and the streaks of soot that traced how the smoke moved through the house.

He led us to the porch, where it all started. In the ashes, we saw what was left of the gas can and the old mattress. Right there was the flash point. All that remained was a massive hole, blown upward at a forty-five-degree angle, straight through the second floor into my brother Matt's room and out through the roof. The fire chief explained how intense the flames had been, and how, even after the fire was out, the smoke kept going, destroying everything it touched.

I could see exactly what he meant. The fire burned things, but the smoke clung to everything—covered and smothered it. It left behind a thick, black film that felt heavier than the flames themselves. As we walked through it all, the house looked like a scene from a horror movie. Everything was dark, charred, and lifeless.

And then, in the middle of it all, we saw it: a single picture hanging on a wall, completely untouched. Everything around it was ruined—scorched, covered in ash—but this one picture was clean as if it had been shielded and protected. It was a cartoon of a pelican trying to swallow a frog, but the frog had its little arms wrapped tightly around the pelican's throat, refusing to go down. Underneath, the caption read: "Never Give Up." We stood there, staring at it. Mom wiped tears from her face; it felt like that picture had been left there for a reason, like a reminder that hope can survive even in the middle of ruin. It was as if the Builder of All Things had left us a sign saying, "I'm still here."

The days and weeks that followed were hard. Facing homelessness, grinding to rebuild, and trying to piece our lives back together wasn't easy. The smell of smoke lingered in the air, a constant reminder of what we'd lost. But that picture stayed with me. It reminded me that no matter how bad the fire, no matter how thick the smoke, there is always hope.

Now, after living through not one, but two, house fires, something had started to shift in me. First, I couldn't help but think about how it all started—how one tiny spark could destroy everything in its path. I'd find myself replaying the scenes in my head, walking through the wreckage, and remembering how the fire chief explained the burn patterns, the heat, and the smoke trails. It was like the house was trying to tell its story, and I couldn't stop wondering why. How did that one tiny moment—the spark—create such a big impact? Not only in the house but in our lives.

Around that time, I started getting inspired by movies like *Backdraft*.[21] Seeing those firefighters run toward the flames, fighting chaos, stirred something inside me. It wasn't just the action. It was about purpose—protecting people, saving what mattered. After our house fires, I couldn't help but think about all the families who had lost everything, just like we did. I knew the feeling of walking through the ashes, smelling the smoke, and realizing that the home you knew was gone. I wanted to do something about it.

At that point, I didn't know how, but the idea stuck with me. When I joined the Navy, firefighting wasn't on my radar, but during boot camp, I was excited to learn it was part of our training. Every recruit had to learn to be a firefighter. We suited up, learned to spot flash points, control flames, and put them out at the source. It wasn't just about extinguishing

---

21 Ron Howard, *Backdraft* (May 24, 1991; Universal City, CA: Universal Pictures).

fires; it was about knowing the science behind them—understanding how they start and spread, and the different colors of smoke that indicate the type of flashover and fire. It felt like a full-circle moment—finally equipping me with the tools and knowledge to fight the thing that had taken so much from my family.

> **JUST LIKE A HOUSE FIRE, THE KEY IS SPOTTING THE DANGER EARLY, KNOWING HOW TO CONTAIN IT, AND BUILDING STRONG SYSTEMS TO PREVENT IT IN THE FIRST PLACE.**

And even though it wasn't why I joined the military, it became one of those unexpected gifts. When I got out of the Navy, I found myself drawn to construction and building homes. It made perfect sense. I'd seen firsthand what happens when a home isn't built right and when small mistakes or neglect can lead to disaster. Building homes felt like a proactive way to protect families before a single spark could ever appear. I wanted to build strong, safe, and reliable homes—places where families could feel secure, knowing their foundation was solid. It wasn't just a job; it was a way to carry that burden I'd felt since those house fires, to act before anyone else had to go through what we did.

But here's where it gets even more interesting. Over time, I started to see the bigger picture. As a business owner now, I know fires don't just happen in houses. In business, in leadership, and in life, we all deal with fires—challenges that can spark and, if left unchecked, grow into full-blown problems. And where there's fire, there's smoke. Maybe it's a bad decision, a hurt team, or ignoring a problem until it's too late. The metaphor became crystal clear: just like a house fire, the key is spotting the danger early, knowing how to contain it, and building strong systems to prevent it in the first place.

As a builder and a business leader, that lesson is at the heart of everything I do. A strong foundation isn't just for homes but for teams, companies, and personal growth. You need structure, early warning systems, and to take care of the small things before they spiral out of control.

Some choices ignite the flame in the furnace to produce smoke that will cover the metaphorical sun and light in your path. I want to expose those moments when the match strikes the substrate right before the flame ignites—what's known as the "flash point."

FLASH POINT

In business, we call this risk management. Let's imagine you have a matchbook, and each match is a choice we could make that would light a fire and create this smoke. The world is a perfect substrate for this so-called match to catch fire, and it can easily create a smoke screen that leads you down the wrong stream.

For you as a leader and business owner, recognizing the smoke means understanding what's happening beneath the surface. You need to know what might be causing the fires in the first place. In my journey, I've identified three high-level key indicators that help me recognize when something is off: Emotional Residue, Ego-Driven Decisions, and Effort Misalignment.

Emotional Residue: Think of it as lingering, unresolved feelings that keep resurfacing. Maybe there's tension among your team members, old hurts and resentments that never got resolved, or personal baggage you're bringing into the office. These unresolved emotions are like little hidden pieces of wood or coal in a fire that can flare up unexpectedly, causing recurring conflicts or personal issues.

Ego-Driven Decisions: We all have pride. We all want to look good, feel important, and be seen as successful. But when ego gets the driver's seat, you start making decisions for the wrong reasons—protecting your image rather than serving the mission. Ego might push you to expand too fast, impress clients or investors with unrealistic promises, or micromanage people to prove you're in control. Before long, you've lit a match.

Effort Misalignment: This is when you're working hard but not working smart. Everyone is busy, but nobody is focused on what matters. Your team might be running around putting out small fires, chasing short-term goals, or focusing on appearance over substance. You're burning energy but not feeding the right priorities. Over time, that friction builds up, and you have a larger fire on your hands.

Spotting these indicators is like being a fire investigator in your own business. Firefighters look for burn patterns. You can do something similar in your company. Maybe look for patterns of conflict. Identify where the biggest losses occurred and ask yourself if ego was involved. Trace the path of failures, missed targets, and confusion to see if it's due to misaligned effort. Each clue leads you closer to the flash point—the moment when something goes from a small spark to a consuming blaze.

CLEARING THE SMOKE

Once you find the flash point, you've got to face it with **Honesty, Humility**, and a commitment to **Healing**. It might mean sitting down for those tough conversations with your team to clear the emotional baggage you've been avoiding. It might mean humbling yourself—admitting you got it wrong, scaling back, and refocusing on what truly aligns with your mission instead of chasing ego-driven goals. Or maybe it's about reevaluating your processes, priorities, and systems to make sure everyone understands the true purpose and that resources are being used wisely.

Think about a solidly built home—it's designed with firebreaks, proper wiring, and materials that can withstand heat. A strong business works the same way. It needs moral and strategic safeguards. When you build a culture of honesty, humility, and purpose, it's like fireproofing your house. When everyone is clear on why the company exists and shares values rooted in something bigger than just profit, those toxic sparks don't catch and spread so easily.

This isn't about shame—it's about awareness. The smoke creeps in quietly, but it doesn't have to take over. If little fires are smoldering in your heart or your business, now's the time to address them. Don't wait until everything's up in flames.

Ask yourself:
1) Where have I seen recurring conflicts?
2) Have I made ego-driven decisions?
3) Is my team expending energy in ways that don't align?

Then, ask the even tougher question: *what's the ignition source?* Like a faulty electrical wire hidden behind a wall or a gas can left on the porch, something sparked the trouble. Maybe you have outdated systems that frustrate your team. Maybe you have a toxic relationship with a client who demands things that compromise your pride. Maybe you've been pushing everyone to deliver unrealistic results, creating a pressure cooker environment. Each of these conditions can set the stage for a moral or operational flash point.

Just as firefighters trace burn patterns and investigate ignition sources—faulty wiring, open flames left unattended, accelerants that made the fire spread faster—you can trace back from your current crisis to the original choice that set it all in motion. Maybe you invested heavily in a product you didn't believe in just to impress investors. Maybe you hired someone who clearly didn't share your values because you were desperate for their skill set. Maybe you ignored red flags in a partnership because you were blinded by the potential payday.

Identifying these ignition points isn't about beating yourself up. It's about learning and rebuilding.

After my family's home burned down, we didn't just slap a coat of paint over the scorched wood and move back in. We had a season of rebuilding. Spiritually and professionally, we must do the same. Rebuild the culture, processes, and priorities. Clear the emotional residue by having honest, healing conversations. Check your ego at the door. Align your efforts with a clear, authentic purpose.

It will take courage. Vulnerability always does. But remember that cartoon picture that encouraged us after the fire—"Never Give Up." Even when the situation looks hopeless or it feels like your business is beyond repair, the Builder of All Things can surprise you. There is hope in humility and changing perspective. There is hope and forgiveness in genuine dialogue. There is hope in learning from your mistakes and setting a new course.

You might wonder, *How do I know if I'm off track?* The truth is, if you're asking that question, you probably already sense that something's wrong. Trust that instinct. Slow down long enough to reflect. In the hustle of business life, it's easy to keep plowing forward, hoping the smoke clears on its own. It rarely does. Instead, slow down and examine the patterns. If you see repeated moral challenges, high employee turnover due to frustration, or a creeping sense of emptiness despite financial success, it's time to pause and investigate.

Consider bringing in trusted mentors, coaches, or spiritual leaders—who can help you see what you might be missing. Sometimes, we're too close to the problem to notice the obvious scorch marks. Like the fire chief who walked my family through the wreckage, pointing out exactly how the flames moved, you need someone with clear vision. Humility is key here. If your ego is defensive, you won't accept help or acknowledge the reality of the damage. But if you can say, "I don't have all the answers," you open the door to wisdom.

> **FIRES HAPPEN. SMOKE WILL APPEAR. THE QUESTION ISN'T WHETHER YOU'LL FACE THESE CHALLENGES; IT'S WHAT YOU'LL DO WHEN YOU SEE THE FIRST SIGN OF SMOKE.**

In practical terms, start small. Identify one lingering emotional conflict in your team and address it openly. Admit one decision you made based more on pride than on principle, and see what happens when you own it. Reassess a project everyone's working hard on but that doesn't tie into your core mission—realign it or let it go. Each step you take clears a bit more of the smoke, allowing you to see the path ahead more clearly.

Let me leave you with a final thought: Fires happen. Smoke will appear. The question isn't whether you'll face these challenges; it's what you'll do when you see the first sign of smoke. Will you ignore it, hoping the wind changes direction? Or will you investigate, face the truth, and extinguish the spark before it becomes a flame?

You have the choice. You can prevent small sparks from igniting big blazes by staying honest and humble. You can make decisions that align with your values, serve your team, and keep your business on a healthy track. And if you've already been through the fire, don't lose hope. Rebuilding is possible. Clarity can return. Purpose can be restored. The smoke can clear, and when it does, you might just find that you're stronger and wiser for having faced it.

This is why I shared this vulnerable chapter—so that my pain and lessons learned wouldn't be wasted and so that you might recognize your own flash points before they cost you everything. May you find the strength and courage to clear the smoke and rediscover the light that was always there, waiting to guide you home. Never Give Up!

> **SONG PAIRING:** "Deconstruction" by Lecrae
> CC4 (Album)[22]

---

22 Lecrae, vocalist, "Deconstruction," by Nathan Robinson, LeCrae Moore, et al., released November 4, 2022, track 13 on *CC4*, Reach Records.

PART 4

BIRTHING THE LEGACY

CHAPTER 9

THE SUN:
All Things New

Power of the Present

"And we know that for those who love God all things work together for good, *for those who are called according to his purpose."*
—Romans 8:28 (ESV)

THE CALM AFTER THE STORM

You've just come through a storm—winds screaming and howling, waves crashing, skies so dark it feels like morning will never come. But then it happens. The sun breaks through. The light spills over the horizon, and everything looks different. The chaos fades, and there's a strange kind of peace in its place. That sunlight doesn't just warm your skin—it recharges your soul. It's a reminder that no matter how bad the trial or adversity, it's temporary. And the sun always rises.

This is the rhythm of life. Storms come to test us, snakes appear to strike when we least expect, and smoke rolls in to cloud our judgment. These challenges are real and often overwhelming, but they don't last forever. After every storm, there's a calm; after every night, there's a dawn.

In my life, I've learned to see these cycles as part of the design. Storms, snakes, and smoke are difficult, but they prepare us for something greater. And when the sun rises again, it doesn't just light up the sky—it fills us with energy, hope, and clarity.

Think of the sun like a plant does. It's fuel. It's power. It's life-giving. Plants stretch toward the light, soaking it in, using it to grow taller and stronger. But they don't stop there. When the night comes, they don't wither away. They survive on what they've stored, knowing the sun will rise again. That's how we're meant to live—drawing energy from the light while being prepared to navigate the darkness.

This chapter is about embracing that cycle. It's about seeing each sunrise as an invitation to grow, each night as a chance to reflect, and every storm as an opportunity to deepen your roots.

JOY IN THE MORNING

While preparing for my new journey into joining the Navy, excitement and anxiety stirred within me. The step I was about to take felt huge, almost overwhelming. At this stage of life, I was fortunate to be aligned with one of my best friends, DeMarco Mason. DeMarco and I had developed a deep bond through our shared experiences on the varsity basketball team throughout high school. During this time, we basically lived together, sleeping at Grandma's, Aunty's, or my parents' house. After high school and our first year of college, we both found ourselves at a crossroads, uncertain of what the future held, but certain that we needed to take the next step in our journey together.

We made the decision to join the "Navy Buddy Enlistment Program," which meant we would go to boot camp together, attend military A school together, and then move on to our duty station together. Knowing that we would have each other's support for the next four years was a comfort we both needed as we stepped into the unknown.

However, before we could move forward, we had to pass multiple tests to be approved for boot camp. I managed to pass all of them, but DeMarco stumbled, failing one of the tests. The timing of everything felt so crucial, and we were both eager to move forward. Our recruiter suggested that DeMarco could retake the test and, if he passed, could join me within thirty days, still as part of the program. So, I went to the Chicago Navy Boot Camp Station and continued my training alone.

During the intense eight weeks of boot camp, I was given just one opportunity to make a phone call. Four weeks later, I called him, and I finally heard DeMarco's voice. He still hadn't been able to start boot camp, but his words were filled with encouragement. His unwavering support meant the world to me, even from afar, knowing he would be joining me soon.

After completing boot camp, I moved on to military A school, where I worked hard and managed to graduate at the top of my class, and as I mentioned earlier, this achievement gave me the rare opportunity to choose my duty station. When I chose Pearl Harbor, Hawai'i, the excitement I felt was indescribable, and when I returned home, I couldn't wait to share the news with my family and friends. But as the days passed, a feeling of resentment began to creep in. I started to feel angry and disappointed when I learned that DeMarco wouldn't be able to join me, and the thought of moving forward without him made me feel isolated.

The night before I was set to leave Peoria to head to my first military duty station in Pearl Harbor, DeMarco unexpectedly showed up at my house. He was full of joy and laughter, and his encouragement that night meant everything to me. He told me how proud he was and assured me he would do everything he could to join me in Hawai'i. His words brought a feeling of peace, and I left with a renewed sense of hope.

My journey to the Hawai'i islands was filled with awe and wonder. My first time going out to sea on a naval warship was an experience I'll never forget. The vastness of the Pacific Ocean stretched out before me, and I spent two months at sea before finally landing in paradise, the tropical island of Oahu, Hawai'i.

A few months passed, and just as I was beginning to settle in, we left for our first six-month deployment. Still no DeMarco. It was a long journey ahead of us before we would reach the Middle East, with stops at many different countries along the way. Before we arrived in Australia, our first stop, I received an email from my grandma, Bonnie. Working in the ship's administrative office gave me access to emails, and as

I read the first few lines, I knew something was wrong. My heart sank, and a sense of dread washed over me. I skimmed through the email, desperate to uncover the source of the tragedy I knew was coming.

DeMarco Mason, my best friend and brother, had been shot multiple times in the chest and head. He had barely reached the hospital when they pronounced him dead. He was gone, just like that.

The world as I knew it shattered. My body went numb, and I couldn't even muster the strength to stand. I looked around, searching for someone, anyone, who might understand the depth of my pain, but I was alone. Alone in the middle of the Pacific Ocean, with no one who knew the bond DeMarco and I had shared. I made my way to the fo'c'sle (forecastle), the front of the ship, where it was quiet and empty at night. My new shipmates, sensing something was wrong, asked me what had happened. I couldn't hold it anymore. I collapsed and wept, their attempts to comfort me unable to touch the depth of my grief.

The days that followed were a blur of pain and confusion. It took time to find meaning and purpose again, and my journey through mourning was long and difficult. I believe now that God had positioned me in the middle of the Pacific Ocean for that moment to go through the loss of my best friend. It was a time of deep reflection and, eventually, a time of healing. Although the mourning lasted for a while, I eventually decided to move forward, to be thankful for the time I had with DeMarco, and to cherish every single moment of my life.

Death has a way of forcing us to see life differently. For a while, I spiraled, lost in my grief. Eventually, I found the strength to change my perspective. It taught me the value of every second, and though the pain of loss will never fully fade, I've learned to carry it with me, a reminder to live each day with purpose and gratitude. DeMarco's passing was a devastating reminder of life's fragility. But even in the midst of that overwhelming grief, I learned to find gratitude in the present. The vast ocean, the endless stars above, and the friendships I formed on that Navy ship became sources of light, teaching me to cherish each moment as a gift. Just like the sun rising after a long night, every day brought a new opportunity for hope.

I've learned through life's challenges that God's promise to make all things new is not just about dramatic transformations but about the small moments we often overlook. Whether it's finding peace after loss, I've learned that the chance to breathe every breath again and again renews me daily. It's about recognizing the fresh opportunities that each day holds. For me, seeing the sun rise each morning is a reminder that I'm still here, still breathing, and that alone is worth appreciating. That's how I know—no matter what—joy really does come with the morning.

> *"Weeping may last through the night,*
> *but joy comes with the morning."*
> —Psalms 30:5 (NLT)

After completing my Navy term and entering the construction world, I carried a hunger to succeed and live out what Demarco couldn't. I'll never forget the lesson I learned on my first day on a construction site. The company owner took notice of my tall build, my work ethic, and the enthusiasm I brought to the job. By the end of that first day, he saw something in me and decided to share a piece of wisdom that's stuck with me ever since. He pulled me aside and pointed out the other carpenters around us, most in their forties and fifties, while I was still just a twenty-year-old kid.

He said:

You see these guys? They've been doing this a long time, and they think they've got it all figured out. But the moment you think you know everything is the moment you stop growing. There's always something new to learn in this world. My advice to you is to keep that mindset. Even when you think you've made it, stay open to learning. The world keeps changing, people keep evolving, and there's always something new out there.

Looking back, I realize I've embraced this mindset in my construction work. It's easy to get caught up in the business growth rush and miss the little moments that make up the journey. After losing DeMarco, it would have been easy to focus solely on the pain. But I realized the Builder of All Things was calling me to something deeper—to appreciate the beauty in each day, in each relationship, and to live fully in the present. It's not easy, but gradually, I've come to realize that even the darkest moments can give way to light.

> **THERE'S A LIMITLESS AMOUNT OF VALUE, WISDOM, AND GROWTH TO BE FOUND IN EVERY TASK WE DO, EVEN WHEN IT FEELS MONOTONOUS.**

Take the story of Jesus feeding five thousand people with just a few loaves of bread and fish. The disciples were at a loss, not knowing how they could possibly feed so many with so little. But Jesus had them gather some baskets, and then He showed them that He had more than enough (see Matthew 14:13-21). That story opened my eyes to how we learn lessons in life. Each challenge, each struggle, each adversity, each success, each win, though it might seem simple or familiar at first, contains an endless supply of wisdom and nourishment. Because He is the source. He is the sun and has provided us with His SON. As you move through life, you might find that a single loaf can keep revealing new insights, offering fresh guidance and understanding, just like the miracle of feeding the five thousand with so little.

I've found that this idea applies even to the most mundane parts of life. In construction, for example, some tasks start to feel repetitive and tiresome. Take installing siding for the exterior of a house, for instance—I've personally experienced that it's often the same materials and motions, repeated over and over, sometimes for what feels like an eternity to complete.

It's easy to get bored and wish you could move on to something more exciting. But just like those loaves of bread and fish that keep on giving, there's a limitless amount of value, wisdom, and growth to be found in every task we do, even when it feels monotonous.

The grass isn't always greener on the other side, and if you're not careful, you might find yourself constantly restless, always looking for something new and exciting while missing the depth and richness of what's right in front of you. If you hold on to the dreams and visions that God places in your heart and step into the journey He has for you, you'll remember that there's an endless stream of fruits along the way, even in the most mundane moments.

> *"He is like a tree planted by streams of water that yields its fruit in its season, and its leaf does not wither."*
> —Psalms 1:3 (ESV)

IF WE CAN APPROACH LIFE WITH THE CURIOSITY OF A CHILD, I BELIEVE WE CAN FIND THE FULFILLMENT AND CONTENTMENT WE'VE BEEN SEARCHING FOR.

Contentment is found in the boat, in the journey itself. The vision we hold is simply there to give our boat direction and keep us moving forward. I've traveled the world and seen countless countries during my Navy tours, and while those destinations were undoubtedly enjoyable, it's the time spent with my shipmates and the bonds we forged during the journey that I'll never forget.

This entire book is meant to shift your perspective, to help you stop focusing solely on the distant horizon, and instead find fulfillment in what's right in front of you. If you can learn to be present—with God, with your journey, and with the people in your life—I promise you that the contentment you seek is already within your grasp. Just as I approach carpentry and my own business, I encourage you to approach life and your business the same way. You may think you know everything about your spouse, parents, siblings, friends, or even colleagues, but approach them with fresh eyes today. Ask your spouse that same old question, "What's your favorite color?" The answer may not have changed, but you might discover something new if you dig a little deeper. And if it's the same color, ask why.

If we can approach life with the curiosity of a child, I believe we can find the fulfillment and contentment we've been searching for. I've been through a lot—from enduring two house fires to losing my best friend to the smaller, yet still significant, challenges of moving to a new house or changing jobs. None of these things lasts forever. What does last are the moments we share with others and the way we choose to appreciate those moments.

Don't take anything for granted—whether it's your parents, spouse, kids, grandkids, or job. Life will always present its challenges, whether they come as smoke, storms, or snakes. I hope that through this book, I've given you some tools to face and overcome these challenges. And when you do, when you're walking the path your purpose has set before you, I believe that behind every storm, every snake, and every haze of smoke lies the sun—a light that will reveal to you your purpose and your reason.

Our role, as stewards of this journey, is to enjoy it. To be present, because the essence of life is found in simply being on the boat. I hope that if your current situation doesn't feel right, remember that it's all about perspective. You are always exactly where you're meant to be in each moment. This moment is your opportunity to shift your viewpoint, board the boat, and choose life.

ALL THINGS WORK TOGETHER

Imagine waking up each morning with a clean slate. Yesterday's chaos doesn't weigh you down, and tomorrow's unknowns don't overwhelm you. It's just you, the day ahead, and the choice to make something of it. When I start my day like that—with the mindset that it's brand new—it changes everything. It allows me to see my wife's beauty with fresh eyes every single day, to feel pride in my children no matter what, to forgive without being shackled by the past, and to take each step with a renewed sense of appreciation for what's right in front of me.

It's not just about staying positive. It's about seeing life as a bigger picture, one where every moment—good or bad—is connected. I live by Romans 8:28 (ESV): "All things work together for good."

What that means to me is that even when life throws curveballs, when things don't go as planned, or when the pressure feels too much, there's value in those moments. They shape us. They push us to grow. And over time, they all piece together into something meaningful, even if we can't see it right away.

Think about the natural world. Rain falls, streams flow into rivers, rivers reach the ocean, and then the water evaporates to start the cycle again. It's a rhythm that might seem repetitive or mundane, but it's essential. It gives life, renewal, and balance. Life works the same way. Sure, daily tasks might feel like a grind—answering emails, solving problems, or managing client expectations. But if you step back and look at the bigger picture, every little thing builds toward something greater. The challenges teach us. The wins remind us why we keep going.

When you embrace this perspective, it changes how you approach everything—your business, your relationships, and even how you see yourself. Believing that everything works together for good doesn't mean pretending life is always smooth. It means understanding that even the hard stuff, even the failures, can work in your favor if you let them. It's about learning, adapting, and finding the purpose behind the process.

As a business owner, this mindset can be a game-changer. When you trust that setbacks aren't the end of the story, you lead with confidence. You become more focused, less reactive, and more creative in how you solve problems. You stop wasting energy on things you can't control and start putting it into what you *can* build.

Here's a practical way to start. Tomorrow morning, before you open your laptop or check your phone, take a moment. Look around. Notice what's good in your life—your family, your team, or even just the fact that you have another day to make an impact. Then, step into your day knowing this: no matter what happens, it's all part of the process.

You might not see how it all fits together yet, but trust me, it does. And when you look back, you'll see that even the hardest moments were setting you up for something greater.

BRIDGING THE GAP

As I speak to you, a business builder, I understand and empathize with the work of your hands—the structures you have to create, the systems you need to put in place, and the vision you have to pour your life into. Yet, I bet there's something more you're seeking. You may call it drive, passion, or purpose, but it feels like a gap, an unanswered question at the foundation of everything you're building.

I see how we can chase success, control, or profit. You honor the hustle, the grind, and the numbers—but there is an unknown Builder of All Things behind it all. The foundation you seek, the purpose you long for, is not an accident of the universe. It is set by the One who made the heavens and the earth.

> **WITHOUT HIM, THE BRICKS AND MORTAR OF YOUR SUCCESS WILL CRUMBLE UNDER THE WEIGHT OF THEIR OWN EMPTINESS.**

This Builder of All Things doesn't dwell in temples or office towers built by human hands. Profit margins, processes, or KPIs don't confine Him, nor does He depend on the work of our hands as though He needs anything from us. On the contrary, He is the One who gives life, breath, and purpose to all things—including your business, your vision, and your very existence.

From one man, He made every nation, every business leader, every entrepreneur. He determined the times set for them, the rise and fall, and the boundaries of their influence. Why? So that we might seek Him, reach out for Him, and find Him—though He is never far from any one of us.

> *"For in him we live and move and exist."*
> —Acts 17:28 (NLT)

Without Him, the bricks and mortar of your success will crumble under the weight of their own emptiness. But with

Him, you will find that you're not just a builder of things—you're a steward of a much greater plan, one that has greater weight and glory.

The question is whether you will align your business with the Builder of All Things. That's the invitation I leave with you: to lay down your blueprints and take hold of His, trusting that His plans are good, His timing is perfect, and His foundation will never fail.

So now, the choice is yours. Will you keep building on your own, or will you join the business partner you didn't know you had? The Builder of All Things. **JESUS.**

Additional Encouragement: *Walk in the sunlight of God's truth with the Son, allowing your satisfaction in Him to guide and illuminate your path.* By aligning with His purpose, you can experience transformation, growth, and a more profound sense of fulfillment in your life.

Author's Note: *Now's the perfect time to jump back into the middle of chapter 10 and wrap things up, if you haven't already.*

> **SONG PAIRING:** "8:28" by Lecrae
> *All Things Work Together* (Album)[23]

---

23 Lecrae, vocalist, "8:28," by Allen Swoope, Austin Owens, et al., released September 22, 2017, track 12 on *All Things Work Together,* Reach Records.

CHAPTER 10

THE SCORE:
We Already Won

Empowered to Live in Freedom

*"For I can do everything through Christ,
who gives me strength."*
—Philippians 4:13 (NLT)

THE UNSEEN VICTORY

In 2020, briefly before COVID-19 swept through the United States, Tiffany and I traveled to Las Vegas for the KBIS (Kitchen and Bath Industry Show) convention. During the trip, we were excited to reunite with some local Hawai'i friends, David and his wife, Robyn. Over the past decade, we had built a strong relationship through involvement at our local church, Inspire Church on Oahu, where we had served as leaders in the youth group together and collaborated on a church mission trip to the Philippines in 2013. We joined for a dinner date that night at a restaurant called Best Friends, which led to some meaningful conversations that I'll never forget. At this dinner, David and I deeply discussed our life journeys since serving together at the church. It was interesting how the Builder of All Things had led us both to write about our encounters and experiences and share them with the world. At that dinner, we mutually committed to each other to write a book, a promise I am now fulfilling. We shared our book ideas and felt compelled to follow through, creating a memorable moment I'll never forget.

Three years later, I invited him to join my podcast to discuss how he maintains his passion, excitement, and joy despite his ongoing personal struggles battling cancer for the third time. He brought up this scripture that continuously guides him: "For I can do everything through Christ, who gives me strength" (Philippians 4:13, NLT).

When I asked him to elaborate, he shared a powerful metaphor drawn from his passion for MMA (Mixed Martial Arts) and martial arts training. He used to pre-record the MMA fights and later peek at who won. If his guy lost, he wouldn't even watch the fight. But if his guy won, he would grab the popcorn, get his family together, and enjoy the whole fight. He then expanded on how that tied into the scripture and what it meant for him. His response resonated deeply with me and inspired me to share my own experience of his perspective, which I'll expand on from here.

I am a devoted fan of the Golden State Warriors, particularly of Stephen Curry, who I've been supporting since his days at Davidson College. I was captivated by his remarkable three-point shooting and ability to score forty-plus points consistently during the NCAA tournaments. As he is only 6' 2" with a small build, it felt like watching a young kid playing against adults. His playing style resonated with me as it mirrored my own style back when I used to play. While I did not have his talent level, his approach to the game strongly caught my attention.

My admiration for Curry grew stronger when he joined the Warriors, and I became a passionate follower of his career. In 2015, my wife and I made a joint decision to pledge to support and root for the Warriors. Coincidentally, that same year, they clinched their first NBA title. Since then, we've remained die-hard fans, eagerly tuning in to every game to this day.

My dedication to the team has been unwavering. Everyone in my family, company, and even our clients all know I'm a Golden State Warriors fan. I make a point not to miss a single game on my Hulu Live subscription, often recording each one to watch later if necessary. Sometimes, the anticipation is so intense that I feel the urge to sneak a peek at the end score. If the Warriors win, I make sure to start from the beginning to watch the entire game and fully enjoy how we pulled off the win.

It has been during these games that I've noticed a shift in my perspective. Regardless of the score going into the final quarter, I've found myself appreciating the moment, assured of our win. This shift has allowed me to savor the journey of the game without being preoccupied by the outcome. I've discovered that knowing the end result in advance has enabled me to appreciate the unfolding events and enjoy the game more deeply.

Now, let's turn to the scriptures David shared during our podcast. His belief in Jesus and eternal life has anchored his outlook, allowing him to embrace life's challenges with hope and optimism. He views life with a sense of assurance—much like the assurance felt in a game scenario when the Warriors are down by twenty points in the fourth quarter with five minutes left, but because we've peeked at the results, we know the ultimate victory has been secured. Regardless of the current score, he knows he has already won!

While most people might view David beating and surviving cancer as a success, in David's eyes, whether he stays on this earth another day or not, he has already won, and his success lies in appreciating every second in the present with his family, meeting Jesus, and securing eternity with Him. I'm so thankful for David! I have recently come to a profound realization of my own after hearing this perspective.

> **OUR INTERNAL BELIEFS AND THOUGHTS HAVE THE POWER TO SHAPE OUR EXTERNAL REALITY.**

One of Jesus's missions during His time on earth was to transform our perspectives and shift our way of thinking, to empower us to live and walk in freedom, and ultimately secure our victory in the afterlife. Paul describes it in the following verses:

> "*Do not conform to the pattern of this world, but be transformed by the renewing of your mind.*"
> —Romans 12:2

> "*For freedom Christ has set us free; stand firm therefore, and do not submit again to a yoke of slavery.*"
> —Galatians 5:1 (ESV)

Another one of my favorite movies is *Inception*, which illustrates the concept of implanting an idea that can alter the entire course of someone's belief system. If you haven't seen this movie starring Leonardo DiCaprio, it's about a thief and his team who steal corporate secrets through dream-sharing technology and are given a task one day that is different from what they are used to. They are asked to plant an idea into the mind of a CEO to alter his perspective and, ultimately, his decisions to keep or break up his father's empire. To pull this off, they have to go deep within a dream of a dream of a dream.[24]

The idea that only one altering thought in our deep belief system could alter everything about the path of our lives intrigued me. This idea doesn't just apply to the movies, it applies to us too. Our internal beliefs and thoughts have the power to shape our external reality. I could easily look at fire as an element that can burn me or as a source of warmth during a cold day, changing my perspective and perception in a matter of seconds.

---

24 Christopher Nolan, *Inception* (July 13, 2010; Burbank, CA: Warner Bros. Pictures).

How we perceive and interpret things in our lives can greatly influence our experience. We have the power to choose how we view situations or things around us, and a shift in perspective can lead to a significant change in our thoughts, feelings, and actions. Look again at the example of the fire; it shows how the same thing can be viewed in different ways. It can be seen as something dangerous or as something comforting, depending on how we choose to look at it.

THE TAMED ELEPHANT

I remember seeing elephants and lions at a circus when they came to town as a kid. They were my favorite to watch because they were the largest and most feared. I was always afraid those massive elephants and fierce lions might escape during the event and come after us—which, in a strange way, made it even more exciting.

Outside the tent, when they staged these animals after the show, I would think, *Why aren't they putting the elephant in a cage like the lion?* An elephant is around 12,000 pounds and one of the largest mammals you'll see walking on land today. They are simply tamed and secured by putting a clamp on their leg with a little chain or rope and a small wooden peg that's placed in the ground. (I'm not sure if they still do this today.)

Surprisingly, the elephant doesn't go anywhere. Isn't that crazy to think about? I've recently learned that from an elephant's perspective, this conditioning starts very young to tame them. At that young age, the peg and the chain are effective because the baby elephant learns that it can't go anywhere when pegged to the ground. The young elephant tries to break free but soon realizes that it isn't possible.

> **THE PERSPECTIVE YOU CHOOSE TO ADOPT CAN KEEP YOU STAGNANT AND CHAINED OR IT CAN SET YOU FREE.**

As the elephant grows older and larger, it stops trying to break free, learning from its previous experience that it is just an impossible task. The elephant's mind is conditioned to believe that the small chain and peg are unbreakable. It doesn't realize that with its adult size, strength, and power, it could easily break the chain and free itself.

I share this tamed elephant story to better understand the power of perspective. The perspective you choose to adopt can keep you stagnant and chained or it can set you free.

As business owners, the way we envision the future of our business is like holding the key to unlock our chains and determine our path forward. It guides every step we take, every choice we make in our marketplace, leading us toward that destination we dream of. But without a clear vision, we're like that elephant held back by a tiny rope, thinking we're moving forward but truly stuck in a loop of stagnation, feeling the weight of purposelessness and stalled growth. It's so important to carve out a powerful vision of where we want to be, to shake off those invisible chains, and to start moving—really moving—toward a life and business fueled by purpose. This vision becomes our compass, guiding us forward with meaning and direction.

I hope to inspire you and remind you of the immense power and strength you hold—like a 12,000-pound elephant. The burdens we carry are undeniably real, but shifting your perspective can be the key to setting yourself free. Just as the elephant needed only to believe it could break free from its chain, we, too, can break the chains that bind us. By changing our perspective from fear of the unknown to confidence in what is known, we unlock our potential.

This chapter presents a profound challenge: to place victory on your path and clarity in your vision for the future. Understanding that the victory is already won and that our paths and callings are predetermined can be deeply empowering. Placing this message at the end of the book while encouraging an advanced sneak peek underscores this sense of assurance—like watching a prerecorded Golden State Warriors game, already knowing the outcome but still marveling at the journey.

As my friend David once said, I truly believe we can do all things through the Builder of All Things, who gives us the strength we need exactly when we need it.

Author's Note: *At this point, you have a choice. If you'd like to see the BLUF ("bottom line up front") right away, feel free to continue ahead and finish chapter 10. Once you've read it, you can come back to chapter 2 and continue the journey.*

Or, if you'd rather take the scenic route and experience each layer as it unfolds, jump back to chapter 2 now and continue to read from there! Both paths lead to the same destination—the way to get there is just different.

A GLIMPSE OF GLORY

It's so important for me to share what my faith means to me and where it comes from because my faith is my vision, my strength, my victory. It's the certainty that when my time on this earth is done, I'll step into eternal life. I know that might sound strange to some, especially if this idea is new or if it's only been heard through the lens of religion. But for me, this promise of eternity is everything. It's the foundation of my faith, and it fuels me through every step of my journey.

Every day, this belief empowers me in my business, knowing that my ultimate victory isn't in temporary achievements but in this unshakable promise. It gives me a confidence I couldn't have on my own because I walk alongside the Creator of everything, my constant partner in every decision. And that same partner, the one who holds eternity, walks with me, guiding and strengthening me through it all.

As people, we are all different in many ways, but there is one thing we can all agree we have in common: one day, we will all face death. Like the baby elephant, we are conditioned to believe that we are not free from death. We find ourselves bound by invisible chains, making decisions as adults with the ticking clock of death looming over us. American culture has set us on this trajectory even further. We are born, go to school and college, have careers, marry, own houses, have families, retire, and one day, we all die. Somewhere around high school and college, the elephant peg syndrome kicks in, and we realize that we are fighting against the clock of death. We start making big decisions and choices to beat time. We need to get a career, get married, have kids, get a house, start a retirement plan, etc.

If only we could change our perspective and recognize the strength and power we possess now, we could break free from these chains, realizing our true calling, and make choices that align with a freedom we all could possess.

Consider for a moment what it would be like to catch a glimpse of the day and circumstances of our death, only to be transported back by a predetermined amount of time. Perhaps a year before that moment. Wouldn't this revelation drastically alter the way we live, think, make choices, and relate to others? This is the kind of profound shift that understanding the end can prompt in us, urging us to live purposefully and invest our time differently.

In March 1983, while living in Peoria, Illinois, I was just three years old when I found myself in a near-death situation and was offered a glimpse of the endgame. My father was asleep in his room, and my nine-month-old baby brother, Matt, was peacefully sleeping in his crib. Meanwhile, my mother had settled me in front of the TV with a bowl of raisin bran cereal before she left for work. Being a typical three-year-old, I accidentally spilled the cereal, and a natural fear kicked in as I knew my spill and mess would upset my parents. I rushed back to my bedroom. Little did I know, the door's locking mechanism could only be engaged from the hallway side, meaning I was locked in the room. I believe my parents set the door up this way to keep us within reach.

In my room, there was a mobile space heater with visible hot coils, a typical device in the cold Peoria winter weather. I recall having this little book with a train of animals circling the back cover, which I decided to place into the heater's hot coils just to see what would happen. Innocently, I placed the book against the heater, lighting its corner like a cigarette, and then watching as it burned out. I repeated this with the next corner, leading to the same result. I got to the final corner of the book to insert, and I accidentally touched the still-hot first corner, burning my hand. Without thinking, I threw the hot book toward the window curtain. Just to give you the full picture, these curtains were made in the seventies. Highly flammable materials. The room was immediately engulfed in flames as the curtains ignited.

The situation quickly spiraled out of control as the fire spread, leaving me no way to escape. Panicking and scared, I attempted to open the door, only to find the doorknob locked and too hot to handle. Smoke filled the air, making it difficult to breathe.

When I heard my nine-month-old baby brother, Matt, crying in his crib, my immediate instinct was to climb in and comfort him. However, my weight caused the crib to break. Fortunately, my brother managed to roll to the ground and put out some of the flames that were burning him. However, he still suffered third-degree burns. Exhausted and overwhelmed, I made my way toward the bed, where a combination of fatigue and smoke inhalation pulled me into unconsciousness, and I fell into a deep, dark void. I remember falling slowly into bed.

Suddenly, a radiant light surrounded me as if I had been transported to a new place. I found myself encircled by a multitude of people. Then, a person emerged from the multitude and started walking toward me. I immediately recognized Him; it was Jesus. Yes, it was Jesus. Let me say it again. It was Jesus!!! Although I can't recall whether He uttered any words or touched me, I remember Him walking up to me. Then, something interesting happened. I woke up to a scene of chaos, as if I were seeing it from a vantage point of thirty feet above the house. It felt like I was floating as I looked down at the fire trucks below, watching my dad step out of the house in a bathrobe and walk to the ambulance.

From that surreal moment, I regained consciousness in the hospital by the side of my grandmother, Bonnie. I shared my encounter with her and expressed how I had seen Jesus. Years later, during my teenage years, my family revealed to me that I had suffered from smoke inhalation and had flatlined at one point, only to be brought back to life in the ambulance on the way to the hospital. This encounter impacted my family and me for the rest of our lives.

Fast forward to my twenties. As a young adult, I visited Peoria for a brief visit from the Navy and had dinner with my dad. I took the opportunity to ask for his version of the experience, as I'd never heard it. As the fire trucks were on their way, my dad made a quick decision to rush into our room, grabbed me and my brother Matt, and hurried us out to the front lawn. He was still asleep when he heard the smoke alarm and moved so fast, without thinking, that he hadn't even put on his robe before rushing out.

As part of our conversation, my father also shared a really interesting new detail that he noticed in the soot and damage when he returned to the room after the fire was put out—unburned footprints imprinted on the carpet, leading from the center of the room toward the bed, where I fell unconscious. This was a powerful affirmation of my experience for me.

FIRE CAPTAIN TREVELYN SMITH is led away from the scene of a fire at 2203 N. Bige- low yesterday morning after suffering smoke inhalation and chest pains.

Peoria blaze injures fireman, two children

Two children and a Peoria Fire Department captain were hospitalized after a blaze yesterday morning at the Richard Breaux residence, 2203 N. Bigelow.

Matthew Breaux, 9 months, and Richard Breaux Jr., 3, both suffered smoke inhalation and were listed in serious condition in the pediatric intensive care unit at St. Francis Hospital. Matthew also suffered second-degree burns on his face, hands and legs.

Fire Capt. Trevelyn Smith, 32, was listed in fair condition at Methodist Medical Center, where he was treated for smoke inhalation. He also complained of chest pains.

Responding to an 8:19 a.m. alarm, firefighters encountered a smoke-filled, one-story wood-frame dwelling with flames in the children's bedroom. It took "only a few minutes to knock down the fire, but the smoke was real bad," said Fire Battalion Chief Pat Malone, who estimated damage at $1,500.

The blaze was caused by a space heater that ignited "unknown combustibles," which then set afire the older child's mattress and carpeting between Richard Jr.'s bed and Matthew's crib, said Fire Investigator John Parker.

The rising flames burned the infant on the right side of his body, while the 3-year-old lay semi-conscious on the smoldering mattress, Parker said.

The fire was discovered by the children's father, who was awakened by a smoke detector in a hallway outside the children's bedroom. Breaux rushed into the room and removed the unresponsive 3-year-old from the hot mattress, Parker said.

Personnel from the fire and police departments arrived and helped the father rescue the baby from the house.

Today, I stand here, heart full and words ready, to share my story of Jesus with you. At just three years old, I had a moment that would shape me forever. A vision of Jesus, surrounded by a multitude of people, radiant in all His glory. It was more than just a sight; it was a glimpse into the victory He promises us. In that moment, I tasted life beyond death, felt the weight of His resurrection, and knew, even as a child, that He had truly conquered death. That memory, that promise, has stayed with me, a constant reminder of the hope and power He offers to each of us.

This encounter has since guided my journey in life with a sense of joy and anticipation, regardless of the obstacles I face. It's a powerful reminder that this perspective makes all the difference regardless of life's ups and downs.

It's been a long time since that pivotal moment, and since then, I've had a profound relationship with Jesus, who rescued me. The core of my testimony rests in the assurance that when we depart from this earth, Jesus will be there among a multitude of people. This understanding has fundamentally transformed my perspective on life and how I approach every day. While I didn't get deep into the Bible until my late twenties, I always held onto a sense of the ultimate victory that Jesus achieved, even when I was uncertain about my purpose and existence.

> **SIGNIFICANCE IS THE CORE STRENGTH THAT DRIVES US TOWARD EMPOWERMENT.**

I was really eager to share this experience with you. It took me a while to open up to people about seeing Jesus at a young age. I was unsure of how people would react to such a personal and potentially debatable story. I do believe it is essential to the overall message in this book and, therefore, important to include in the final chapter.

Now, you might wonder, *What does this have to do with building a business or finding my purpose?* My hope, the goal of this book, is for you to find real significance in what you're doing. Sure, we all find purpose in our work in one way or another but discovering significance? That's the game changer. It shifts your perspective in a way that lasts forever.

Significance is the core strength that drives us toward empowerment. Significance is the "why" behind your purpose. Picture your business as the boat and your purpose as the stream you're moving along. It can move and has direction but significance? That's the rudder, God's hand guiding the boat forward. He's steering us through every twist and turn, keeping us on course. And the real beauty is that God's hand is what gives us the deepest, truest significance. He's the one making sure that every step we take, every move we make, is part of a purpose bigger than ourselves. Significance is knowing your work counts toward something bigger than just you. That's where real joy and fulfillment come from; it's what gives your purpose that deeper meaning that sticks around.

Imagine you're on a construction crew building a community center. It's hot, the work is physically hard, and you're sore. Now, if you're just there for a paycheck, it's easy to get frustrated and think, *Why am I even doing this?* But let's say you know that this building is going to be a safe place for kids after school or a shelter for people who need it. Now, it's not just about pouring concrete or framing walls; it's about giving something meaningful to the community. That's your significance.

When you start to see it that way, you feel that drive kick in. You're not just working for the day or the week—you're building something that's going to impact lives. That's why you dig deeper and push through the hard days, knowing you're part of something bigger than yourself.

Deep down, I believe we all crave a sense of purpose, meaning, and a reason for being. Some of us may have yet to fully experience that feeling, but when you find it, something awakens, as if your spirit recognizes, "This is what I was made for." We were created for that yearning, crafted to pursue something greater.

On my journey, I've found a vision to build a company in the construction market that sets a new standard of excellence. It's given me and our team a purpose and a solid path to walk. But the real significance is the calling to serve and lead, pushing our industry to change for the better. It's about creating a way of doing things that raises the bar, something that eventually leaves a legacy, a new standard for other construction companies to follow.

> **BELIEVING IN JESUS OPENS THE DOOR TO AN AFTERLIFE WHERE WE OVERCOME DEATH.**

Every step I take is filled with intention and significance, aligning my work with how I was created to be. The desire to please, to serve, to build something meaningful flows in harmony with the way God has guided and built me all along. This is the heart of fulfillment. Merging your deepest desires with your work and purpose, letting them unfold.

It all comes back to Jesus. I want to emphasize that He is real, and He is alive. I aim to be a messenger to assure you that in the end, we've already won through Him. Believing in Jesus opens the door to an afterlife where we overcome death.

I hope to inspire you and remind you again of the immense power and strength you hold—like a 12,000-pound elephant. The burdens we carry are undeniably real, but shifting your perspective can be the key to setting yourself free. Just as the elephant needed only to believe it could break free from its chain, we, too, can break the chains that bind us. By changing our perspective from fear of the unknown to confidence in what is known, we unlock our potential.

Jesus invites each of us to break free, change our perspective from the unknown to the known, and believe. Interestingly, the essence of repentance is to simply change your perspective to Him as the key to eternal life.

Embrace the symbolism of the elephant breaking free from its chains, recognizing that through Jesus's sacrifice to die on the cross, resurrect from the grave, and defeat death, we are now free from the bondage of death through Him. His resurrection teaches us that our choices no longer need be dictated by fear of death but by the promise of life.

> *"So Christ has truly set us free. Now make sure that you stay free, and don't get tied up again in slavery to the law."*
> —Galatians 5:1 (NLT)

I know you may think that you haven't seen Jesus or had any kind of crazy revelation that would give you this kind of belief or assurance.

In both Matthew 8:5-13 and Luke 7:1-10, there is the story of a Roman soldier during Jesus's time on earth. He was a military officer who wasn't part of the Jewish community but had a deep respect and compassion for the people around him. One day, his servant became ill, and the soldier was desperate to help. He'd heard of Jesus and believed that, somehow, this teacher and healer could save his servant. He felt unworthy to approach Jesus himself, so he sent a group of Jewish elders to ask Jesus for help on his behalf. They vouched for him, telling Jesus about his leader's kindness and generosity.

As Jesus made his way to the soldier's home, the soldier sent another message, full of faith. He told Jesus he didn't need to come all the way to his house. Instead, he believed that if Jesus simply *spoke* a word, his servant would be healed. He compared Jesus's authority to his own, saying that just as he could command soldiers, Jesus had the power to command healing.

When Jesus heard this, he was amazed. He turned to the crowd following him and said he hadn't seen such great faith, not even in Israel. Jesus then granted the soldier's request, and the servant was healed without Jesus even stepping into the soldier's home.

This story captures a beautiful mix of humility and faith. The soldier's faith wasn't just about belief; it was grounded in a deep understanding of authority and respect, paired with his unwavering trust in Jesus's power, even from a distance.

I hope and pray that you might have the same faith. Now that you have read my story, I encourage you to walk forward in life, knowing that Jesus is indeed alive and offers real hope. Be a part of the generation whose faith is so unwavering that it would amaze even Jesus, for believing in Him, without the tangibility of seeing Him, is the truest affirmation of faith.

The final score of life's game can already be settled in our favor and grace through Jesus. By recognizing this truth and aligning our actions accordingly, we can live a life stamped with confidence, purpose, and significance. *It's not about striving for victory but living from a place of victory,* allowing it to shape our decisions, relationships, and contributions to the world.

> **SONG PAIRING:** "I Still Believe" by Lecrae feat. For King + Country[25]

---

25 Lecrae, vocalist, "I Still Believe," by Tedd Tjornhom, Joel David Smallbone et al., released March 1, 2024, single, Reach Records.

If you're ready to take the next step in your journey with the Builder of All Things, don't let this moment pass you by. Follow this podcast, join the movement, and become part of a community that's driven to build something greater. Together, we're not just talking about change—we're living it. Let's rise, inspire, and move forward with purpose. Your journey starts here.

ABOUT THE AUTHOR

Born in Peoria, Illinois, Richie Breaux's life was forever changed at age three when a house fire shook his world and brought him face-to-face with Jesus. From that moment, his life was marked by purpose. After relocating to California and then back to Peoria, his family faced yet another devastating house fire that resulted in the loss of everything. Despite these hardships, Richie thrived as a three-star athlete in high school, which eventually led him to play college football. However, it was God's calling that guided him to enlist in the Navy, where he was stationed in Pearl Harbor, Hawai'i.

In Hawai'i, Richie met Tiffany, the love of his life. Together for more than 20 years, they have shared over 17 years of marriage, raised four children, and welcomed 13 grandchildren. In 2012, they took a leap of faith to start a residential construction company in Hawaii, beginning with limited resources and humble beginnings. Through steadfast trust in God, Richie and Tiffany grew the business, doubling its revenue year after year, earning recognition in 2021 as one of the fastest-growing companies in the nation, and securing a spot on the Inc. 5000 list as well as the Top 50 Construction Companies in the U.S.

Richie's journey extends far beyond business success. In 2020-24, his leadership was recognized on Hawaii's Business Top 250 Business list and in the Black Book of top executives to know in Hawai'i. In 2021, he was honored as one of the National Kitchen and Bath (KBB) Persons of the Year. In 2023, his company made headlines by leading the renovation of one of the highest-selling homes in Orange County, which sold for $34 million and was purchased by Chicago Bulls star Zach LaVine, further establishing his reputation as one of the nation's top builders.

Beyond construction, Richie is a dedicated advocate for improving the industry, collaborating with government agencies to bring about meaningful change. As a life coach, business consultant, and empowerment leader, he helps others unlock their potential and pursue their callings. In 2024, Richie was named a Modern Man by Modern Luxury Magazine, positioning him to redefine leadership in his community.

Richie Breaux's journey has left a lasting impact on the construction industry and the lives of many, cementing his legacy as a visionary leader in Hawai'i.

I want to personally invite you to take a practical step toward getting well and eliminating stress from your life. Scan the QR code now and join me at The Well Club—a place designed to equip you with real-world tools, insights, and encouragement. Let's walk this journey together, reducing stress, finding balance, and living your best life, starting today.

Scan the code and let's get well—together.

If not now ... when?
—Richie Breaux

www.ingramcontent.com/pod-product-compliance
Lightning Source LLC
Chambersburg PA
CBHW070530090426
42735CB00013B/2927